The Life and Adventures of Nat Love

The Life and Adventures of Nat Love

A True History of Slavery Days

Nat Love

MINT EDITIONS

The Life and Adventures of Nat Love: A True History of Slavery Days was first published in 1907.

This edition published by Mint Editions 2021.

ISBN 9781513208855 | E-ISBN 9781513293554

Published by Mint Editions®

MINT
EDITIONS

minteditionbooks.com

Publishing Director: Jennifer Newens
Design & Production: Rachel Lopez Metzger
Project Manager: Micaela Clark
Typesetting: Westchester Publishing Services

CONTENTS

Preface

Having passed the half century mark in life's journey, and yielding to persistent requests of many old and valued friends of the past and present, I have decided to write the record of slave, cow-boy and pullman porter will prove of interest to the reading public generally and particularly to those who prefer facts to fiction, (and in this case again facts will prove stranger than fiction). I assure my readers that every event chronicled in this history is based on facts, and my personal experiences, of more than fifty years of an unusually adventurous life.

While many things contained in this record happened many years ago, they are as fresh in my memory as if they happened but yesterday. I have tried to record events simply as they are, without attempting to varnish over the bad spots or draw on my imagination to fill out a chapter at the cost of the truth. It has been my aim to record things just as they happened, believing they will prove of greater interest thereby; and if I am able to add to the interest and enjoyment of a single reader I will consider myself well repaid for the time and labor of preparing this history.

To my playmates of my boyhood, who may chance to read this I send greetings and wish them well. To the few friends, who assisted myself and widowed mother in our early struggles, I tender my sincerest thanks, and hope they have prospered as they deserve. For those who proved our enemies, I have no word of censure. They have reaped their reward.

To that noble but ever decreasing band of men under whose blue and buckskin shirts there lives a soul as great and beats a heart as true as ever human breast contained—to the cow-boys, rangers, scouts, hunters and trappers and cattle-men of the "Great Western Plains," I extend the hand of greeting acknowledging the Father-Hood of God and the Brotherhood of men; and to my mother's Sainted name, this book is reverently dedicated.

The Author

I

SLAVERY DAYS. THE OLD PLANTATION. MY EARLY FORAGING.
THE STOLEN DEMIJOHN. MY FIRST DRINK.
THE CURSE OF SLAVERY.

In an old log cabin, on my Master's plantation in Davidson County in Tennessee in June, 1854, I first saw the light of day. The exact date of my birth I never knew, because in those days no count was kept of such trival matters as the birth of a slave baby. They were born and died and the account was balanced in the gains and losses of the Master's chattels, and one more or less did not matter much one way or another. My father and mother were owned by Robert Love, an extensive planter and the owner of many slaves. He was in his way and in comparison with many other slave owners of those days a kind and indulgent Master.

My father was a sort of foreman of the slaves on the plantation, and my mother presided over the kitchen at the big house and my Master's table, and among her other duties were to milk the cows and run the loom, weaving clothing for the other slaves. This left her scant time to look after me, so I early acquired the habit of looking out for myself. The other members of father's family were my sister Sally, about eight years old, and my brother Jordan, about five. My sister Sally was supposed to look after me when my mother was otherwise occupied; but between my sister's duties of helping mother and chasing the flies from Master's table, I received very little looking after from any of the family, therefore necessity compelled me at an early age to look after myself and rustle my own grub. My earliest recollections are of pushing a chair in front of me and toddling from one to the other of my Master's family to get a mouthful to eat like a pet dog, and later on as I became older, making raids on the garden to satisfy my hunger, much to the damage of the young onions, watermelons, turnips, sweet potatoes, and other things I could find to eat. We had to use much caution during these raids on the garden, because we well knew what we would catch if someone caught us, but much practice made us experts in escaping undetected.

One day when Master and the family went to town mother decided to make some wine of which she was very fond, accordingly she gathered some grapes and after pressing them she made some fairly good wine.

This she placed in a demijohn, and this for better security she hid in the garden, as she thought unknown to anyone, but my brother, sister and myself had been watching the process with considerable curiosity, which finally reached such a pitch that there was nothing to it; we must sample a liquid that looked so good. So Jordan went to the hay loft from where a good view could be obtained all around, while myself and Sally busied ourselves in the vineyard. Presently Mother thinking all secure left the house with the demijohn and proceeded to hide it. Jordan, from the hay loft, noted that mother never left the garden until she returned to the house, empty handed, but he was unable to see the exact hiding place.

It was several days later while passing through the garden that we ran across the lost demijohn. It did not take us long to discover that its contents suited our tastes. Sally and Jordan dragged it into a sweet corn patch, where we were safe from observation. An oyster can was secured to serve as a glass and the way we attacked that wine was a caution to the Temperance Workers. And I can assure you we enjoyed ourselves for a while, but for how long I am unable to tell exactly. Mother soon missed us but being very busy she could not look for us until evening, when she started out to look us up, after searching and calling in vain. She decided to take the dogs to help find us. With their aid we were soon located, lying in the sweet corn, "dead drunk," while the demijohn quite empty, bottom side up, stared at mother with a reproachful stare, and the oyster can which had served up and took me to the house, and let Sally and Jordan lie in near by, bearing mute witness against us. Mother picked me up and took me to the house, and let Sally and Jordan lie in the sweet corn all night, to dwell on the events. Immediately preceding our return to consciousness is a painful subject to me as it was exceedingly painful then. I was most feverish the next day with a head on my shoulders several sizes larger than the one I was used to wearing. Sally and Jordan were enjoying about the same health as myself, but the state of our health did not exempt us from mother's wrath. We all received a good sound old-fashioned thrashing. A fitting prelude to my first "drunk."

I suppose I acquired the taste for strong drink on this occasion; be that as it may, the fact remains that I could outdrink any man I ever met in the cattle country. I could drink large quantities of the fiery stuff they called whiskey on the range without it affecting me in any way, but I have never been downright drunk since that time in the sweet corn patch. Our plantation was situated in the heart of the black belt of the south, and on the plantations all around us were thousands of slaves, all engaged in garnering the dollars that kept up the so-called aristocracy of the south, and many of the proud old families owe their standing and wealth to the toil and sweat of the black man's brow, where if they had to pay the regular rate of wages to hire laborers to cultivate their large estates, their wealth would not have amounted to a third of what it was. Wealth was created, commerce carried on, cities built, and the new world well started on the career that has led to its present greatness and standing in the world of nations. All this was accomplished by the sweat of the black man's brow. By black man I do not mean to say only the black men, but the black woman and black child all helped to make the proud south what it was, the boast of every white man and woman, with a drop of southern blood in their veins, and what did the black man get in return? His keep and care you say? Ye gods and little fishes! Is there a man living today who would be willing to do the work performed by the slaves of that time for the same returns, his care and keep? No, my friends, we did it because we were forced to do it by the dominant race. We had as task masters, in many instances, perfect devils in human form, men who delighted in torturing the black human beings, over whom chance and the accident of birth had placed them. I have seen men beaten to the ground with the butts of the long whips carried by these brutal overseers, and for no other reason than that they could not raise to their shoulders a load sufficient for four men to carry. I have seen the long, cruel lash curl around the shoulders of women who refused to comply with the licentious wishes of the men who owned them, body and soul—did I say soul? No, they did not own their soul; that belonged to God alone, and many are the souls that have returned to him who gave them, rather than submit to the desires of their masters, desires to which submission was worse than death. I have seen the snake-like lash draw blood from the tender limbs of mere babies, hardly more than able to toddle, their only offense being that their skin was black. And young as I was my blood often boiled as I witnessed these cruel sights, knowing that they were allowed by the laws of the land in which I was born. I used to think it was not the country's fault, but the fault of the men who made the laws. Of all the curses of this fair land, the greatest curse of all was the slave auction block of the south, where human flesh was bought and sold. Husbands were torn from their wives, the baby from its mother's breast, and the most sacred commands of God were violated under the guise of modern law, or the law of the land, which for more than two hundred years has boasted of its freedom, and the freedom of its people.

Some of the slaves, like us, had kind and indulgent masters. These were lucky indeed, as their lot was somewhat improved over their less fortunate brothers, but even their lot was the same as that of the horse or cow of the present day. They were never allowed to get anything in the nature of education, as smart negroes were not in much demand at that time, and the reason was too apparent, education meant the death of the institution of slavery in this country, and so the slave owners took good care that their slaves got none of it.

Go and see the play of "Uncle Tom's Cabin," and you will see the black man's life as I saw it when a child. And Harriett Beecher Stowe, the black man's Saviour, well deserves the sacred shrine she holds, along with the great Lincoln, in the black man's heart.

II

When I was ten years old the war broke out between the "North and the South." And there was little else talked about, among the slaves as well as the slave owners of the neighborhood. And naturally the many different stories we heard worked us children to a high state of excitement. So much so that we wanted to go to war, and fight for the Union, because among us slave children there was no difference of opinion, as to which side was right.

The Union was "It," and we were all "Yankees." Not being able to go to war as our masters did, we concluded to play war, accordingly I gathered all the boys of the neighborhood together, into a regiment, which it was my intention to divide into two parties of Rebels and Yankees, but in this I met an insurmountable obstacle. Not one of the boys wanted to be a rebel, consequently we had to look elsewhere for an enemy to give us battle, and serve as a vent for our growing enthusiasm. The next Sunday preceding the organization of our regiment, we started out over the surrounding country in quest of trouble, which we were not long in finding, as we soon ran across a nest of yellow jackets. These we proceeded to exterminate, in which we were successful after a short but destructive battle. We suffered considerably in wounded but lost none of our soldiers. This engagement we called the capture of fort "Hell." For some time thereafter we made regular raids into the surrounding country in quest of an enemy. We were eventually successful in our quest, as in quick order we ran across and captured a company of bumble bees. This we called the "Battle of the Wilderness." Victory over a nest of hornets we called the capture of "Fort Sumter." A large nest of wasps gave us perhaps the hardest fight of our campaigning. This we ran across in the fields not far from home. There was an unusually large number of them, and as is usually the case with these insects, they proved very ferocious. Nothing loth, however, we attacked with cheers, only to be driven back time and again and finally we were compelled to make a very undignified retreat, at full speed in the direction of home. Not to be beaten, however, we secured reinforcements and more ammunition, in the shape of old rags, brooms and so forth, and returned to the charge, and although we were driven back several times we stayed until we won out, and the last insect lay a quivering mass on the ground. There was not one among us, not wounded in some manner, as for myself I had enough of it. My nose looked like a dutch slipper, and it was several days before my eyes were able to perform the duties for which they were made. However, the Union forces were victorious and we were happy. Our masters told us if the soldiers caught us, they would hang us all, which had the effect of keeping most of us close around home. Master had gone to join Lee's forces, taking with him father, who was engaged in building forts, which work kept him with the Confederate army until General Grant arrived in the country, when he was allowed to come home. From then on Union soldiers passed the neighborhood most every day on their way south, to join the fighting regiments.

We soon found out they would not hurt us and they were the wonderment and pride of our youthful minds. They would take everything they could find to eat for themselves and horses, leaving the plantation stripped clean of provisions and food, which entailed considerable misery and hardships on those left at home, especially the colored people, who were not used to such a state of affairs and were not accustomed to providing for their own wants. Finally Lee surrendered and master returned home. But in common with other masters of those days he did not tell us we were free. And instead of letting us go he made us work for him the same as before, but in all other respects he was kind. He moved our log cabin on a piece of ground on a hill owned by him, and in most respects things went on the same as before the war. It was quite a while after this that we found out we were free and good news, like bad news, sometimes travels fast. It was not long before all the slaves in the surrounding country were celebrating their freedom. And "Massa Lincoln" was the hero of us all.

While a great many slaves rejoiced at the altered state of affairs; still many were content to remain as before, and work for their old masters in return for their keep. My father, however, decided to start out for himself, to that end he rented twenty acres of land, including that on which our cabin stood, from our late master.

We were at this time in a most destitute condition, and father had a very hard time to get a start, without food or money and almost naked, we existed for a time on the only food procurable, bran and cracklins. The limited supply of provisions made the culinary duties most simple, much to the disgust of mother, who was one of the best cooks in the country, but beggars cannot be choosers, and she very cheerfully proceeded to make the best of what we had. She would make a great fire in the large fire place in the cabin. The fire when hot enough, was raked from the hearth and a small place cleaned away, in the center of this clean space, mother would lay a cabbage leaf, on which she would pour some batter made from bran and water or buttermilk and a little salt. Then on top another cabbage leaf was laid and hot coals raked over the whole, and in a short time it would be baked nicely. This we called ash cake.

This, with occasional cracklins made up our entire bill of fare for many months. Father would make brooms and mats from straw and chair bottoms from cane and reeds, in which my brother and I would help him, after he had taught us how. During the week a large load was made and Friday night father would take the load on his shoulders and walk to town, a dozen miles, where he would sell them and bring seed and food home. When the weather would permit we worked in the field, preparing for our first crop.

The twenty acres, being mostly uncultivated, had to be cleared, plowed and thoroughly harrowed. Our first crop consisted of corn, tobacco and a few vegetables.

Father would lay off the corn rows. Jordan and I would drop the corn while father came behind and covered the rows.

In this manner we soon had in a considerable crop of corn and some vegetables for our own use. During the winter which was sometimes severe, during which time nothing, of course, could be done in the farming line, and when not otherwise engaged, we started to try and learn ourselves something in the educational line. Father could read a little, and he helped us all with our A B C's, but it is hard work learning to read and write without a teacher, and there was no school a black child could attend at that time. However, we managed to make some headway, then spring came and with it the routine of farm work. Father was a man of strong determination, not easily discouraged, and always pushing forward and upward, quick to learn things and slow to forget them, a keen observer and a loving husband and father. Had he lived this history would not have been written.

III

RAISING TOBACCO, OUR FIRST YEAR OF FREEDOM.
MORE PRIVATIONS. FATHER DIES. IT NEVER RAINS—
BUT IT POURS. I BECOME THE HEAD OF THE FAMILY
AND START TO WORK AT $1.50 PER MONTH.

A s soon as the corn crop was in the ground we commenced to plant tobacco. Before the seed was sown, it was necessary to gather large piles of brush and wood and burn it to ashes on the ground to destroy the seeds of the weeds. The ground was then spaded and raked thoroughly, and the seed sown. After it had come up and got a fair start, it was transplanted in rows about three feet apart. When the plants become large enough it is necessary to pull the suckers off, also the worms off the leaves. This task fell upon Jordan and myself.

In picking the worms off the plants it is necessary to use the greatest care that the plants are not damaged, but Jordan and I were afraid to touch the worms with our fingers, so we took sticks and knocked them off, also a few leaves with each worm. This fact called forth some rather strong language from father, who said we were doing more harm than good. But our aversion to the worms was so strong that we took several thrashings before we could bring ourselves to use our fingers instead of a stick. When the tobacco was ripe there would be yellow spots on the leaves. It was then cut, let lie for one day, then hung on a scaffold to be sun cured. It was allowed to remain on the scaffold for perhaps a week, then it was hung up in the barn to be smoked, after which it was made into a big bulk and a weight placed on it to press it out, then it was stripped, and put into hands and then it was ready for the market. Our crop the first year was not large and the most of it went to pay the rent and the following winter proved a hard one, and entailed considerable privation and suffering among the many ex-slaves, who had so recently been thrown on their own resources, without money or clothing or food, and only those who have had the experience can appreciate the condition of things or rather lack of things, at the close of the war, and these conditions did not only affect the ex-slaves and colored people, but covered the entire south, and many former well-to-do slave owners now found themselves without a penny they could call their own, having been stripped of everything and compelled to start all over again. Surely "war is hell"—but slavery is worse. Early in the spring father went to work for a neighboring planter a couple of weeks in order to get his plows and horses again to plow his land. A somewhat larger crop was put in this year, but unfortunately for us when everything was planted father took sick and died shortly after. This was a stunning loss to us just at a time when we most needed a father and husband's help, counsel and protection. But we did not lose courage for long.

The crop must be looked after and the coming winter provided against. My sister Sally had been married about three years at this time and was with her husband and two little girls on a small farm some distance away, which my brother-in-law rented. That left mother, Jordan and I to look after things. Although I was the youngest, I was the most courageous, always leading in mischief, play and work. So I now took the leadership, and became the head of the family. Things were beginning to take on a more hopeful look, when my brother-in-law died, leaving my sister sick with two small children and in about the same circumstances as ourselves. Everything, indeed, looked hopeless now, as our late master and his brother had left the old place and gone north. So remembering I was the only man on the place now, though only fifteen years old, I said to mother and sister who were weeping bitterly, "brace up, and don't lose your heads. I will look after you all." I said this with a bravado I was far from feeling, but I could not see the use of weeping now; there was work to be done, if we were to keep from starving the coming winter. We all turned in to help one another and in this manner. The crop was gathered and we were in fairly good condition for the coming winter, but the work was too much for Sally who lingered through the winter and early in the spring we laid her beside her father and husband, and her two little orphans were left to us. It now became very apparent to me that something must be done, because the crop raised the year before was barely enough to last us through the winter and we would soon be in actual need again. We needed clothing, especially the little girls of my sister, and we had no money to buy seed for this season's crop or food to last us out. So I concluded to go to work for some one if I could find anything to do. With that resolve, I put on my best rags and to mother's inquiry as to where I was going I told her I did not know myself. It fairly made my heart ache to see my little nieces going around almost naked, bare footed, and have them always asking for things I was powerless to give them. I determined to go from place to place until I secured employment of some kind that would in a measure, permit me to feed, and as far as I was able, clothe mother and the children, now dependent on me.

The fact that I was now free, gave me new born courage to face the world and what the future might hold in store for me. After tramping around the country for two days, I finally secured work with a Mr. Brooks, about six miles from home at one dollar and fifty cents a month. Notwithstanding the smallness of my prospective wages, I was happy and returned home in a jubilant frame of mind, to impart the news to mother. I was to commence the next morning. Mother said it was not much, but better than nothing. I told mother that I thought I could bring some food and clothing home for the children before the month was out. The little ones hearing this, were overjoyed and looked on me as a rich man indeed. Jordan was to remain at home and attend to what little there was to do, and the next day I started work for Mr. Brooks. In less than a week I made my first visit home, taking with me some potatoes, bacon, cornmeal, and some molasses, which I had rustled in various ways. I also had a bundle of old clothing given to me by the neighbors, which mother could make over for the children, and to say the children were happy is but a mild expression.

For the second month I received a raise of fifty cents, and the third month of my employment, so good did I work, that I received three dollars. With so many at home to provide for, my wages did not last long, but out of my three dollars I bought each of the children a book. The rest went for provisions and clothing. One day while passing the store of Mr. Graves, near our home I saw a checked sunbonnet and a red calico dress which struck my fancy as just what I wanted for mother. On asking the price Mr. Graves told me I could have the sunbonnet for twenty-five cents and the dress for four bits. That seemed to be within my means, and quite reasonable. I asked him to keep them for me until I got my wages at the end of the month. This Mr. Graves promised to do if I would pay him something down. I only had fifteen cents of which I paid five cents on the bonnet and ten cents on the dress and went on my way, filled with happy thoughts as the result of my bargain. I resolved to be very saving this month and I became very impatient for my month to end and was continually asking Mr. Brooks if my month was not soon over. He would laugh and say "yes, soon." But it seemed to me that was the longest month I ever knew. When at last the month was over he gave me fifty cents, claiming I had drawn my wages during the month. I knew that was not so. I also knew I had a balance coming to me and told him so. But he denied it and the result was that we had a fight. I hit him in the head with a rock and nearly killed him after which I felt better. Then going to Mr. Graves the storekeeper, I told him the whole trouble. He expressed sympathy for me and said to give him the fifty cents and take the bonnet and dress, and we will call it square. And you can imagine my feelings as I took the things home to mother, and she was more pleased with them than any queen with her silks and satins. There being plenty of work to do at home, I did not again look for other work. The only thing that worried me was that the little ones were still without shoes, but on my promise to soon get them some they were satisfied. It was here I got my first lessons in self-dependence and life's struggles. I learned true usefulness and acquired the habit of helping others which I carried with me all through my after life and that trait perhaps more than any other endeared me to my companions on the range and all with whom I have had dealings.

IV

BOYHOOD SPORTS. MORE DEVILMENT. THE ROCK BATTLES.
I HUNT RABBITS IN MY SHIRT TAIL. MY FIRST EXPERIENCE
IN ROUGH RIDING. A QUESTION OF BREAKING
THE HORSE OR BREAKING MY NECK.

I n those days it was more the custom, than now, to work six days and
rest on the seventh, accordingly us boys always had our Sundays free.
And we never lost an opportunity to put in motion some devilment
to make the time pass in what we thought was the most pleasant way.
Anything to have a great time. Our chief means of having fun for a
while was the rock battles. We boys of the entire neighborhood would
get together, then divide in equal numbers on a side, then after gathering
all the available rocks from the landscape, we would proceed to have a
pitched battle, throwing the rocks at each other as hard as we could,
and with a grim intent to commit battery. As a rational consequence
the bravest would force the weaker side to retreat. It then became a
question of running or being rocked to death. After these battles we
were all usually in very bad condition, having received very hard knocks
on sundry and various parts of our anatomy, but for all that we have
never bore malice toward each other. We were careful to keep these
escapades from the knowledge of our elders. In this way we were quite
successful until one time we had a boy nearly killed, then we thought
the old folks would whip us all to death. This incident ended the rock
battles. But we soon had something else doing to furnish ourselves fun
and excitement.

About this time we planned a rabbit hunt, after the small cotton tail
rabbits, which were plentiful in the surrounding country. Getting all
the boys together and securing the track hounds of the neighborhood
we were off. It was not long before the dogs caught track of something
and away they went with all the boys behind. Now at that time it was
not customary for us boys of the plantation to wear shoes and pants, the
principal reason being that we did not have either shoes or pants to wear.
So you can perhaps imagine the sight presented by a score or more of
boys of all ages chasing behind the hounds, with our shirt tails flying
through bushes, thorns and brambles, up hill and down hill, many of us
bleeding like stabbed pigs, but we were too much interested to pay any

attention to a little blood. We wanted the rabbits, and everything else was of secondary importance, even the calls of the younger boys who got tired and fell behind. Onward we went over rocks, through fields, over fences, until we could hear the dogs no more, then tired out we had to stop. I told the boys to sit down, that I thought the dogs would come this way again. It was not long before I thought I heard something and told the boys to hush and have their rocks ready to kill the rabbit. It never occurred to me that it would be anything but a rabbit. The bay of the dogs came nearer, then over the fence jumped a big red fox right in front of me. He stopped and we looked in each others eyes. It was hard to tell which of us was the most surprised, however, I was the first to run away, and run I did. I ran like a black tailed deer. Many times I thought I felt him nibble at my shirt tails, and his eyes grew in my imagination as large as wagon wheels and Mr. Fox, himself, seemed to grow as big as an elephant. When at last I dropped from sheer exhaustion and could summon courage to look behind me, I could see nothing. It was then I realized I was not so game as I thought I was and the knowledge was not pleasant by any means. Not far from our house there was a horse ranch, owned by a Mr. Williams. He had two sons about my own age and I would often go and see them on Sundays. As I was very fond of riding horses most of the horses on the ranch were very wild. So one day the oldest boy and I made a plan to break the young colts. The only chance we had of doing so was on Sunday, when the family went to church, as we did not think Mr. Williams would approve of our plan. Mr. Williams' boy said he would give me ten cents for every colt I broke. That was perfectly satisfactory to me. The money was made of shin plaster those days (paper). The next Sunday I started to break horses. We did not dare to put the bridle on them as we were afraid the boss might surprise us and we would not be quick enough to get it off. Our mode of procedure was to drive one at a time in the barn, get it in a stall, then after much difficulty I would manage to get on its back. Then the door was opened and the pole removed and the horse liberated with me on its back, then the fun would commence. The colt would run, jump, kick and pitch around the barn yard in his efforts to throw me off. But he might as well tried to jump out of his skin because I held on to his mane and stuck to him like a leech. The colt would usually keep up his bucking until he could buck no more, and then I would get my ten cents. Ten cents is a small amount of money these days, but in those days that amount was worth more to me than ten dollars now.

Well, we went on Sunday after Sunday and I broke about a dozen colts in this way, and also managed to do it without the boss discovering the favor I was undoubtedly doing him, in breaking all his wild horses. Only his boys were aware of the doings and they paid me. So I had no scruples about what I was doing, especially as it afforded me great fun. Finally the boys wanted me to break a big handsome black horse called Black Highwayman. Knowing the horse's uncertain temper and wild disposition and taking into consideration its size, I refused to break him for ten cents, as the fact was I was rather scared of him. After considerable bargaining, in which I held out for fifty cents, we finally compromised on twenty-five cents. But I can assure you it was more for the money than the fun of the thing, that I finally consented to ride him. With great difficulty we managed to get him in a stall as we did the others, but I no sooner landed on his back than he jumped in the manger with me hanging to his mane. Finally the door was opened and the pole removed and out of the barn we shot like a black cloud, around the yard we flew, then over the garden fence. At this juncture the track hounds became interested and promptly followed us. Over the fields we went, the horse clearing the highest fences and other obstacles in his way with the greatest ease. My seat on his back was not the most comfortable place in the world, but as the horse did not evince any disposition to stop and let me get off, I concluded to remain where I was. All the dogs of the neighborhood were fast joining in the race and I had quite a respectable following. After running about two miles we cleared a fence into a pasture where there was a large number of other horses and young colts, who promptly stampeded as we joined them, Highwayman taking the lead with me on his back, looking very much like a toad. And all the dogs in the country strung out in the rear. Naturally we formed a spectacle that could not fail to attract the attention of the neighbors, who soon as possible mounted horses and started in pursuit and vainly tried to catch my black mount but could get nowhere near him, while I without bridle or anything to control him could do nothing but let him run as all the other horses bunched around us and the dogs kept up a continual din. I simply held on and let him go. It was a question of breaking the horse or breaking my neck. We went over everything, through everything, until finally the killing pace told and Black Highwayman fell, a thoroughly exhausted and completely conquered and well broken horse. As for myself, I was none the worse for my exciting ride. But on looking for my twenty-five cents,

I found it gone. The boys had paid me in advance, as I insisted, and I had tied the money up in a corner of my shirt tail and during my wild ride it had come untied and worked out. This was a great misfortune to me and for a while I was inconsolable. I asked the boys if they would make it right, but no, they had paid me once and they refused to give me another quarter. This riled me considerable and I told them all right, to come again when they wanted a horse broken. That settled us and the horse breaking. The experiences I gained in riding during these times, often stood me in good stead in after years during my wild life on the western plains. Mr. Williams of course, heard of my last wild ride, but instead of being angry, he seemed to see the funny side of it, which I could not.

The spectators wondered how in the world I ever escaped a broken neck and I have often wondered how I escaped in after years from situations that seemed to be sure death. But escape I did and am now hale and hearty, without pain, with muscles like iron and able at any time to run a hundred yards in eleven seconds or jump a six foot fence.

V

HOME LIFE. PICKING BERRIES. THE PIGS COMMIT LARCENY.
NUTTING. WE GO TO MARKET. MY FIRST DESIRE TO SEE THE
WORLD. I WIN A HORSE IN A RAFFLE. THE LAST OF HOME.

I now settled down to the work around the farm and the problem of making a living for those dependent on me. The crop was all in and after attending to such work around home as had to be done, we found a source of revenue in gathering berries for market. Large quantities of black berries and others grew wild in the woods near by. And they always found a ready market. With small pails and a big basket mother and I would start out after the work at home was done. Reaching the woods we would sit under the bushes and fill the pails, then empty them into the big basket until that was full which usually comprised our day's work,

One day, wishing to secure a large quantity of berries for market, we went early in the morning and on reaching the woods we placed the big basket in what we thought a safe place, and after some hours of industrious work, the big basket was full of nice ripe blackberries. We then proceeded to fill our pails again which would be sufficient for the day. This accomplished, we prepared to start for home. But when mother went to take the big basket it was empty.

The stray pigs had found them and committed larceny. Mother felt so bad she cried. We had put in a hard day's work for nothing. It had been our intention to take them to town on the morrow and buy something for Sunday, but now the fruit of our labor was gone and the disappointment was great. I looked at mother, then at the empty basket and did not know for which to feel most sorry. So I said, "Well, there is no use grieving over spilt milk. If we had not had them we could not have lost them, and there are plenty more of the same kind for the picking." Mother turned toward me and said, with a look I will always remember, "My boy, whatever happens, you never get discouraged." I did not see the use of losing courage and I think the only time I weakened was when father died, as he could not be replaced.

We went on talking and picking berries, and before we knew it the basket was full again and the pails. It was now night so mother took the bushel basket on her head and I took the pails and we were soon home. That night mother took my clothing, as was customary, and washed and pressed it so I would look nice and clean to go to market the next day. As I only had one outfit of clothes I had necessarily to go without them during the washing process, however, mother always kept me clean, at considerable labor on her part. The next morning, early, mother and I started for town, five miles distant, walking along the hot, dusty road, each of us with a basket of berries on our heads and bunches of cucumbers in our hands, mother having much the larger load, but she was a very strong woman. As it chanced we had a lucky day and sold our stock of berries and cucumbers in a short time. We then bought what we needed and had a little money left but for all that, I was not quite satisfied. I wanted mother to buy something that was not necessary, but she said, "My son, if we don't save a few cents now what will it be later on? We will have to go to the poorhouse." I said, "Dear mother if there is a house poorer than ours I don't want to see it." I will always remember the sight of mother's face as she turned to me, the tears running down her cheeks as she answered, "Yes, my son, you are right there are few houses poorer than ours now." The same year when fall came mother and I thought we had the bull by the horns. There were several fine groves of walnut, hickory nut, chestnut and shirly bark nut trees in the woods and I made a sleigh on which I nailed a big box. I tied a rope for a tongue and with a stick on the end, mother and I working as a sort of double team would draw through the woods among the trees gathering the different kinds of nuts and as the box was big, large quantities could be gathered in this manner. During the nut season we worked every day from morning to night, gathering large quantities of nuts for which we always found a ready market. As we worked we talked of what we would buy with the money and making plans for the future. The nuts we sold usually brought us: chestnuts one dollar a bushel; walnuts fifty cents, and hickory nuts fifty cents a bushel. This money added to the proceeds of the crop netted us quite a nice sum and made our condition much better, but I assure you, dear readers, it took hard work from morning to night to make both ends meet but with the help of God we made them meet, and during this time we were always healthy and the knowledge that we were free and working for ourselves gave us courage to continue the struggle. It was about this time that I commenced thinking about going west.

I wanted to see more of the world and as I began to realize there was so much more of the world than what I had seen, the desire to go grew on me from day to day. It was hard to think of leaving mother and the children, but freedom is sweet and I wanted to make more of the opportunity and my life than I could see possible around home. Besides I suppose, I was a little selfish as mortals are prone to be. Finally the desire to go out in the world grew so strong that I mentioned it to mother, but she did not give me much encouragement, and I don't think she thought I had the courage to go, and besides I had neither clothing or money and to tell the truth, the outlook was discouraging even to me, but I continued to look for an opportunity which happened in a very unexpected manner shortly after. One day a man by the name of Johnson announced that he would raffle a fine beautiful horse at fifty cents a chance. I heard of it at once, but had no money with which to get a chance. However, when there's a will there's a way, so I went to the barn and caught two chickens which I sold for fifty cents and at once got a chance. My chance won the horse. Mr. Johnson said he would give me fifty dollars for the horse and as I needed the money more than the horse I sold the horse back. Mr. Johnson at once raffled him off again and again I won the horse, which I again sold for fifty dollars. With nearly a hundred dollars I went home and told mother of what I had done and gave her half of the money, telling her I would take the other half and go out in the world and try and better my condition. I then went to town and bought some underwear and other needful articles, intending to leave at once, but mother pleaded with me so hard to stay home, that I finally consented to remain one more month, but at the end of that time she pleaded for one more and I could not refuse her. During this time my uncle came to live with us and I asked him to take my place at home. This he consented to do gladly. Things were going on fairly well at home now. The farm was yielding a fair living and the children having grown much larger they were a source of help instead of an hindrance and now that my uncle and my brother Jordan were home to look after mother, I felt I could better leave them now, because I was not really needed at home. After gathering what few things I wanted to take with me and providing myself with some needed clothes, I bade mother and the old home farewell, and started out for the first time alone in a world I knew very little about.

VI

I t was on the tenth day of February, 1869, that I left the old home, near Nashville, Tennessee. I was at that time about fifteen years old, and though while young in years the hard work and farm life had made me strong and hearty, much beyond my years, and I had full confidence in myself as being able to take care of myself and making my way.

I at once struck out for Kansas of which I had heard something. And believing it was a good place in which to seek employment. It was in the west, and it was the great west I wanted to see, and so by walking and occasional lifts from farmers going my way and taking advantage of every thing that promised to assist me on my way, I eventually brought up at Dodge City, Kansas, which at that time was a typical frontier city, with a great many saloons, dance halls, and gambling houses, and very little of anything else. When I arrived the town was full of cow boys from the surrounding ranches, and from Texas and other parts of the west. As Kansas was a great cattle center and market, the wild cow boy, prancing horses of which I was very fond, and the wild life generally, all had their attractions for me, and I decided to try for a place with them. Although it seemed to me I had met with a bad outfit, at least some of them, going around among them I watched my chances to get to speak with them, as I wanted to find some one whom I thought would give me a civil answer to the questions I wanted to ask, but they all seemed too wild around town, so the next day I went out where they were in camp.

Approaching a party who were eating their breakfast, I got to speak with them. They asked me to have some breakfast with them, which invitation I gladly accepted. During the meal I got a chance to ask them many questions. They proved to be a Texas outfit, who had just come up with a herd of cattle and having delivered them they were preparing to return. There were several colored cow boys among them, and good ones too. After breakfast I asked the camp boss for a job as cow boy. He asked me if I could ride a wild horse. I said "yes sir." He said if you can I will give you a job. So he spoke to one of the colored cow boys called Bronko Jim, and told him to go out and rope old Good Eye, saddle him and put me on his back. Bronko Jim gave me a few pointers and told me to look out for the horse was especially bad on pitching. I told Jim I was a good rider and not afraid of him. I thought I had rode pitching horses before, but from the time I mounted old Good Eye I knew I had not learned what pitching was. This proved the worst horse to ride I had ever mounted in my life, but I stayed with him and the cow boys were the most surprised outfit you ever saw, as they had taken me for a tenderfoot, pure and simple. After the horse got tired and I dismounted the boss said he would give me a job and pay me $30.00 per month and more later on. He asked what my name was and I answered Nat Love, he said to the boys we will call him Red River Dick. I went by this name for a long time.

The boss took me to the city and got my outfit, which consisted of a new saddle, bridle and spurs, chaps, a pair of blankets and a fine 45 Colt revolver. Now that the business which brought them to Dodge City was concluded, preparations were made to start out for the Pan Handle country in Texas to the home ranch. The outfit of which I was now a member was called the Duval outfit, and their brand was known as the Pig Pen brand. I worked with this outfit for over three years. On this trip there were only about fifteen of us riders, all excepting myself were hardy, experienced men, always ready for anything that might turn up, but they were as jolly a set of fellows as on could find in a long journey. There now being nothing to keep us longer in Dodge City, we prepared for the return journey, and left the next day over the old Dodge and Sun City lonesome trail, on a journey which was to prove the most eventful of my life up to now.

A few miles out we encountered some of the hardest hail storms I ever saw, causing discomfort to man and beast, but I had no notion of getting discouraged but I resolved to be always ready for any call that might be made on me, of whatever nature it might be, and those with whom I have lived and worked will tell you I have kept that resolve. Not far from Dodge City on our way home we encountered a band of the old Victoria tribe of Indians and had a sharp fight.

These Indians were nearly always harrassing travelers and traders and the stock men of that part of the country, and were very troublesome. In this band we encountered there were about a hundred painted bucks all well mounted. When we saw the Indians they were coming after us yelling like demons. As we were not expecting Indians at this particular time, we were taken somewhat by surprise.

We only had fifteen men in our outfit, but nothing daunted we stood our ground and fought the Indians to a stand. One of the boys was shot off his horse and killed near me. The Indians got his horse, bridle and saddle. During this fight we lost all but six of our horses, our entire packing outfit and our extra saddle horses, which the Indians stampeded, then rounded them up after the fight and drove them off. And as we only had six horses left us, we were unable to follow them, although we had the satisfaction of knowing we had made several good Indians out of bad ones.

This was my first Indian fight and likewise the first Indians I had ever seen. When I saw them coming after us and heard their blood curdling yell, I lost all courage and thought my time had come to die. I was too badly scared to run, some of the boys told me to use my gun and shoot for all I was worth. Now I had just got my outfit and had never shot off a gun in my life, but their words brought me back to earth and seeing they were all using their guns in a way that showed they were used to it, I unlimbered my artillery and after the first shot I lost all fear and fought like a veteran.

We soon routed the Indians and they left, taking with them nearly all we had, and we were powerless to pursue them. We were compelled to finish our journey home almost on foot, as there were only six horses left to fourteen of us. Our friend and companion who was shot in the fight, we buried on the plains, wrapped in his blanket with stones piled over his grave. After this engagement with the Indians I seemed to lose all sense as to what fear was and thereafter during my whole life on the range I never experienced the least feeling of fear, no matter how trying the ordeal or how desperate my position.

The home ranch was located on the Palo Duro river in the western part of the Pan Handle, Texas, which we reached in the latter part of May, it taking us considerably over a month to make the return journey home from Dodge City. I remained in the employ of the Duval outfit for three years, making regular trips to Dodge City every season and to many other places in the surrounding states with herds of horses and cattle for market and to be delivered to other ranch owners all over Texas, Wyoming and the Dakotas. By strict attention to business, born of a genuine love of the free and wild life of the range, and absolute fearlessness, I became known throughout the country as a good all around cow boy and a splendid hand in a stampede.

After returning from one of our trips north with a bunch of cattle in the fall of 1872, I received and accepted a better position with the

Pete Gallinger company, whose immense range was located on the Gila River in southern Arizona. So after drawing the balance of my pay from the Duval company and bidding good bye to the true and tried companions of the past three years, who had learned me the business and been with me in many a trying situation, it was with genuine regret that I left them for my new position, one that meant more to me in pay and experience. I stayed with Pete Gallinger company for several years and soon became one of their most trusted men, taking an important part in all the big round-ups and cuttings throughout western Texas, Arizona and other states where the company had interests to be looked after, sometimes riding eighty miles a day for days at a time over the trails of Texas and the surrounding country and naturally I soon became well known among the cowboys[,] rangers, scouts and guides it was my pleasure to meet in my wanderings over the country, in the wake of immense herds of the long horned Texas cattle and large bands of range horses. Many of these men who were my companions on the trail and in camp, have since become famous in story and history, and a braver, truer set of men never lived than these wild sons of the plains whose home was in the saddle and their couch, mother earth, with the sky for a covering. They were always ready to share their blanket and their last ration with a less fortunate fellow companion and always assisted each other in the many trying situations that were continually coming up in a cowboy's life.

When we were not on the trail taking large herds of cattle or horses to market or to be delivered to other ranches we were engaged in range riding, moving large numbers of cattle from one grazing range to another, keeping them together, and hunting up strays which, despite the most earnest efforts of the range riders would get away from the main herd and wander for miles over the plains before they could be found, overtaken and returned to the main herd.

Then the Indians and the white outlaws who infested the country gave us no end of trouble, as they lost no opportunity to cut out and run off the choicest part of a herd of long horns, or the best of a band of horses, causing the cowboys a ride of many a long mile over the dusty plains in pursuit, and many are the fierce engagements we had, when after a long chase of perhaps hundreds of miles over the ranges we overtook the thieves. It then became a case of "to the victor belongs the spoils," as there was no law respected in this wild country, except the law of might and the persuasive qualities of the 45 Colt Pistol.

Accordingly it became absolutely necessary for a cowboy to understand his gun and know how to place its contents where it would do the most good, therefore I in common with my other companions never lost an opportunity to practice with my 45 Colts and the opportunities were not lacking by any means and so in time I became fairly proficient and able in most cases to hit a barn door providing the door was not too far away, and was steadily improving in this as I was in experience and knowledge of the other branches of the business which I had chosen as my life's work and which I had begun to like so well, because while the life was hard and in some ways exacting, yet it was free and wild and contained the elements of danger which my nature craved and which began to manifest itself when I was a pugnacious youngster on the old plantation in our rock battles and the breaking of the wild horses. I gloried in the danger, and the wild and free life of the plains, the new country I was continually traversing, and the many new scenes and incidents continually arising in the life of a rough rider.

VII

I Learn to Speak Spanish and Am Made Chief
Brand Reader. The Big Round-ups. Riding
the 7-Y-L Steer. Long Rides. Hunting Strays.

Having now fairly begun my life as a cowboy, I was fast learning the many ins and outs of the business, while my many roamings over the range country gave me a knowledge of it not possessed by many at that time. Being of a naturally observant disposition, I noticed many things to which others attached no significance. This quality of observance proved of incalculable benefit to me in many ways during my life as a range rider in the western country. My employment with the Pete Gallinger company took me all over the Pan Handle country, Texas, Arizona, and New Mexico with herds of horses and cattle for market and to be delivered to other ranch owners and large cattle breeders. Naturally I became very well acquainted with all the many different trails and grazing ranges located in the stretch of country between the north of Montana and the Gulf of Mexico, and between the Missouri state line and the Pacific ocean. This whole territory I have covered many times in the saddle, sometimes at the rate of eighty or one hundred miles a day. These long rides and much traveling over the country were of great benefit to me, as it enabled me to meet so many different people connected with the cattle business and also to learn the different trails and the lay of the country generally.

Among the other things that I picked up on my wanderings, was a knowledge of the Spanish language, which I learned to speak like a native. I also became very well acquainted with the many different brands scattered over this stretch of country, consequently it was not long before the cattle men began to recognize my worth and the Gallinger company made me their chief brand reader, which duties I performed for several years with honor to myself and satisfaction to my employers. In the cattle country, all the large cattle raisers had their squad of brand readers whose duty it was to attend all the big round-ups and cuttings throughout the country, and to pick out their own brands and to see that the different brands were not altered or counterfeited. They also had to look to the branding of the young stock.

During the big round-ups it was our duty to pick out our brand, and then send them home under the charge of our cowboys, likewise the newly branded stock. After each brand was cut out and started homeward, we had to stay with the round up to see that strays from the different herds from the surrounding country did not again get mixed up, until the different home ranges were reached. This work employed a large number of cowboys, who lived, ate and often slept in the saddle, as they covered many hundreds of miles in a very short space of time. This was made possible as every large cattleman had relays of horses sent out over the country where we might be expected to touch, and so we could always count on finding a fresh horse awaiting us at the end of a twenty-five or a fifty mile ride. But for us brand readers there was no rest, we merely changed our saddles and outfit to a fresh horse and were again on the go. After the general round up was over, cowboy sports and a good time generally was in order for those engaged in it. The interest of nearly all of us centered in the riding of what was known as the 7 Y-L steer. A big long horn wild steer, generally the worst in the herd, was cut out and turned loose on the open prairie. The cow boy who could rope and ride him would get the steer as his reward, and let me assure you dear reader, that it was not so easy as it sounds, as the steer separated from its fellows would become extremely ferocious and wild, and the man who attempted to rope and ride him would be in momentary danger of losing his life, if he relaxed in the least his vigilance and caution, because a wild steer is naturally ferocious. Even in cutting them out of the round up I have known them to get mad and attack the cowboys who only saved themselves by the quickness of their horses, or the friendly intervention of a comrade who happened to be near to rope the maddened long horn, and thus divert his attention to other things. But in the case of the 7 Y-L steer such intervention is against the rules, and the cowboy who attempts to rope and ride the steer must at all times look out for himself. I have seen two horses and their riders gored to death in this sport, and I have had to shoot more than one steer to save myself and horse after my horse had fallen with me and placed himself as well as me at the maddened beast's mercy. At such times it takes a cool head and a steady hand as no random shot will stop a wild steer. The bullet must be placed in a certain spot, the center of the forehead to accomplish its mission. The last time I had a horse fall with me in roping the 7 Y-L steer, he fell as the steer was but a few feet away, falling in such a way that my leg caught under the saddle, holding me fast. Quick as I could I gave the steer a bullet in the head and he stumbled and fell dead on top of my horse and me, so that the boys had to interfere to the extent of dragging the steer and horse off of my leg.

The cowboy who is successful in roping the steer must then mount and ride him. If he does that successfully the steer becomes his personal property to do with as he will, only a slight reward for the risking of his life and the trouble of accomplishing the feat. But it is done more for sport's sake than anything else, and the love of showing off, a weakness of all cow boys more or less. But really it takes a high class of horsemanship to ride a long horn, to get on his back and stay there as he runs, jumps, pitches side ways, backwards, forward, up and down, then over the prairie like a streak of lightning. I have had the experience and I can assure you it is no child's play. More than one 7 Y-L steer has fallen to my lot, but I had to work for it, and work hard. After all it was only part of the general routine of the cow boy's life, in which danger plays so important a part. It is seldom thought of being merely a matter of course, and none of us would have foregone the sport, had we known that sure death awaited us as the result, because above all things, the test of a cow boy's worth is his gameness and his nerve. He is not supposed to know what fear means, and I assure you there are very few who know the meaning of that word.

Most of my readers no doubt have heard of the great round ups and cuttings, connected with the cattle raiser's life. But not one in a hundred has any idea as to how an immense herd of wild cattle are handled in a big round up. My many years of experience has given me unusual knowledge on the subject, and you may bring any cattleman or boss to me, and I will guarantee to answer any question he can ask me about the cattle business. The first general round up occurs about the first of April. This round up is to run in all the near cattle belonging to each man, and head them toward our respective ranges. If we find any other brand mixed up with ours we head them toward their own range, and keep our own together. Every cow boy does the same and in this way every cattleman is enable to get his own brand together on his own range, so that when the next general round up occurs he will have most of his near cattle together on the home range. In order to get the cattle together in the first general round up, we would have to ride for hundreds of miles over the country in search of the long horn steers and old cows that had drifted from the home range during the winter and were now scattered to the four winds of heaven. As soon as they were found they were started off under the care of cow boys for the place agreed upon for the general round up, whether they belonged to us or not, while the rest of us continued the search. All the cow boys from the many different outfits working this way enabled us to soon get all the strays rounded up in one great herd in which the cattle of a dozen different owners were mixed up together. It then became our duty to cut out our different herds and start them homewards. Then we had to brand the young stock that had escaped that ordeal at the hands of the range riders. On finding the strays and starting them homewards, we had to keep up the search, because notwithstanding the fact that we had done range riding or line riding all winter, a large number of cattle would manage to evade the vigilance of the cow boys and get away. These must all be accounted for at the great roundup, as they stood for dollars and cents, profit and loss to the great cattle kings of the west. In going after these strayed and perhaps stolen cattle we boys always provided ourselves with everything we needed, including plenty of grub, as sometimes we would be gone for nearly two months and sometimes much longer. It was not an uncommon occurrence for us to have shooting trouble over our different brands. In such disputes the boys would kill each other if others did not interfere in time to prevent it, because in those days on the great cattle ranges there was no law but the law of might, and all disputes were settled with a forty-five Colt pistol. In such cases the man who was quickest on the draw and whose eye was the best, pretty generally got the decision. Therefore it was of the greatest importance that the cow boy should understand his gun, its capabilities and its shooting qualities. A cow boy would never carry anything but the very best gun obtainable, as his life depended on it often. After securing a good gun the cow boy had to learn how to use it, if he did not already know how. In doing so no trouble or expense was spared, and I know there were very few poor shots on the ranges over which we rode and they used the accomplishment to protect themselves and their employer's cattle from the Indian thiefs and the white desperadoes who infested the cattle country, and who lost no opportunity to stampede the herds and run off large numbers of them. Whenever this happened it generally resulted in a long chase and a fierce fight in which someone was sure to get hurt, and hurt badly. But that fact did not bother us in the least. It was all simply our duty and our business for which we were paid and paid good, and so we accepted things as they came, always ready for it whatever it might be, and always taking pride in our work in which we always tried to excel.

Christmas, Dec. 25, 1872, is a day in my memory which time cannot blot out. I and a number of friends were in a place called Holbrook, Ariz. A dispute started over a saddle horse with the following result. Arizona Bob drew his forty-five Colt revolver, but before he had time to fire he was instantly killed by A. Jack. Then a general fight ensued in which five horses and three men were killed.

It was a sad thing for me to see my friends dead in a corral on a Christmas morning, but I helped bury the dead and took care of the wounded. The names were A. Jack, Wild Horse Pete and Arizona Bill.

VIII

ON THE TRAIL. A TEXAS STORM. A CATTLE STAMPEDE. BATTLE
WITH THE ELEMENTS. AFTER BUSINESS COMES PLEASURE.

After the round ups and on returning from our long rides after strayed cattle we would have to prepare to take the trail with herds of cattle and horses for market and to be delivered to other large ranch owners. The party of cow boys to make these trips were all selected men. We would spend several days at the home ranch resting up and preparing our outfit, in which our guns, saddles, blankets and horses were given a thorough overhauling and placed in first class condition, as they would be called on to do good hard service on these trips on the trail. The nature of our journey would depend very much on the kind of cattle we were called upon to handle. Sometimes it would be all classes together; on other occasions the herd would consist of a certain kind, such as long yearlings, short yearlings, tail end and scabs. The larger demand however, seemed to be for straight three and four year old steers. These latter kind were the easiest to handle on the trail. It is no doubt necessary that I explain the difference between the different kinds I mention here. Short yearlings were those over one year old and short of two years, long yearlings those two years and short of three years, tail end and scabs mean nearly the same thing, and comprise all the very young stock of all classes not yet reached the dignity of yearlings. These latter were in demand from the cattle men, who took them to feed until they got their growth or to raise from, as stock cattle three or four years old were generally the market or beef cattle. These latter were by all odds the easiest to handle on the trail. Sometimes we would have an order for five or six hundred head of all classes of cattle, then again we would have to start out with fifteen hundred head of shipping steers, or several hundred head of horses.

Shortly after I entered the employ of the Pete Gallinger company, and after the round-ups of the early season, we received an order for two thousand five hundred head of three year old steers to be delivered at Dodge City, Kansas. This was the largest herd I had up to the present time followed good rest at the home ranch, we strung the large herd out with two months provisions, and the camp wagon. After a and one hundred extra saddle horses and several pack horses, on the trail. Our outfit consisted of forty picked cow boys, along the old Chillers trail en route for Kansas, and we started on what proved to be an eventful journey. The herd behaved splendidly and gave us very little trouble until we crossed the Red river and struck the Old Dog and Sun City trail, here they became restless, and stampeded nearly every night, and whenever they got half a chance. This made it very hard on us cowboys, as it is no easy matter to ride the lines of such a large herd, let alone having to chase them back in line from many miles over the prairie where they had stampeded in their wild career. After crossing the Kansas line at a place known as the South Forks, while making for the head of the Cimarron river on the twenty-seventh of June, we experienced one of the hardest rain and hail storms I had ever seen, in the western country, the rain came down in torrents only to cease and give place to hail stones the size of walnuts. While the thunder and lightning was incessant. It was shortly after dark when the storm commenced. The twenty-five hundred head of cattle strung out along the trail became panic stricken and stampeded, and despite our utmost efforts, we were unable to keep them in line.

Imagine, my dear reader, riding your horse at the top of his speed through torrents of rain and hail, and darkness so black that we could not see our horses heads, chasing an immense herd of maddened cattle which we could hear but could not see, except during the vivid flashes of lightning which furnished our only light. It was the worst night's ride I ever experienced. Late the next morning we had the herd rounded up thirty miles from where they started from the night before. On going back over the country to our camp of the night before, we saw the great danger we had been in during our mad ride. There were holes, cliffs, gulleys and big rocks scattered all around, some of the cliffs going down a sheer fifty feet or more, where if we had fallen over we would have been dashed to pieces on the rocks below, but we never thought of our personal danger that night, and we did not think particularly of it when we saw it further than to make a few joking remarks about what would have happened if some one of us had gone over. One of the boys offered to bet that a horse and rider going over one of those cliffs would bring up in China, while others thought he would bring up in Utah. It was our duty to save the cattle, and every thing else was of secondary importance. We never lost a single steer during this wild night—something we were justly proud of. This proved the last trouble we were to have with the herd, and we soon reached the five mile divide, five miles from Dodge City without further incident, and with our herd intact. Here we were to hold them until turned over to their new owners. This accomplished, our work was done and done well for this trip. Then we all headed for Dodge City to have a good time, and I assure you we had it. It was our intention and ambition to paint the town a deep red color and drink up all the bad whiskey in the city. Our nearly two months journey over the dusty plains and ranges had made us all inordinately thirsty and wild, and here is where we had our turn, accordingly we started out to do the town in true western style, in which we were perfectly successful until the town had done us, and we were dead broke. This fact slowed us up, because being broke we could not get up any more steam and we had to cool down right there. We then started out to find our boss, but that gentleman being wise in his time and generation, and knowing we would soon all be broke, and would be wanting more money, and that he would let us have it if we asked him for it only to be thrown away, he made himself scarce, and he kept out of our sight until we cooled off. For my part I would not spend all my money. I would draw about fifty dollars, then I would get what things I wanted and then would let the other go free, but while our money lasted we would certainly enjoy ourselves, in dancing, drinking and shooting up the town. It was our delight to give exhibitions of rough riding roping and everything else we could think of to make things go fast enough to suit our ideas of speed. After several days spent in this manner we would begin to make ready to start on the return journey home to Texas. We left Dodge City on the first of July and on the fifteenth of August we were back on the old home ranch, where we rested up a few days before again starting out to ride the range after the long horns again. As I was a brand reader I had little time to rest as my services were in demand from many of the large cattle kings of Texas and Arizona, and when ever a dispute arose over brands, I was generally sent for to straighten matters out. This with the numerous round ups which I had to attend and the many transfers of cattle throughout the pan handle country kept me continually on the go. When my services were not needed as a brand reader I rode the range along with the other cow boys. This kept us almost continually in the saddle, and away from the home ranch for days at a time; when this was the case our food consisted of biscuit and cakes which we made ourselves from meal which we carried with us, and such meat and game as we could knock over with our guns. We camped wherever it suited and where there was feed for our horses. A cow boy's first care is always after his gun and his horse, that animal often meaning life and liberty to the cow boy in a tight place and the cow boy without a horse is like a chicken without its head, completely lost. My faithful horse has times without number carried me out of danger and preserved my life. We were not destined to have much rest this season as shortly after we returned from the trip to Dodge City, the boss bought a large herd of cattle down on the Rio Grande, just over the line in Mexico, which we had orders for, so we had to start out and round them up. This was no easy matter as they were scattered over a large range of territory and many strays had to be rounded up and got with the main herd. This we finally accomplished, after a great deal of hard riding over the rough Rio Grande country, and both men and horses were completely tired out, so we went into camp, only holding the herd together and getting rested up. This opportunity we improved by getting acquainted and fraternizing with the cow boys of one of the oldest cattle countries this side of the herring pond—Old Mexico. These men were for the most part typical greasers, but they proved to us that they knew a thing or two about the cattle business, and all things considered they were a jolly companionable sort of an outfit. From them we learned a few pointers and also gave them a few very much to our mutual benefit. We remained here a few days before starting northward with our herd, but these few days proved very pleasant ones to us boys who, on account of the monotony of the life we led always welcomed new experiences or events that would give us something to think and talk about while on our long rides behind the slow moving herd of long-horn steers, or around our camp fires when in camp on the plains, and it gave us especial pleasure to meet men of the same calling from other states over the west. It not only gave us pleasure, but it added to our cow knowledge, and of the country over which we might at any time be called on to drive cattle, and in such cases a knowledge of the country was most valuable to us. Then a cow boy's life contains many things in which he is continually trying to improve and excel, such as roping, shooting, riding and branding and many other things connected with the cattle business. We, in common with other trades, did not know it all, and we were always ready to learn anything new when we met any one who was capable of teaching us.

IX

En Route to Wyoming. The Indians Demand Toll.
The Fight. A Buffalo Stampede. Tragic Death of Cal.
Surcey. An Eventful Trip.

After getting the cattle together down on the Rio Grande and both man and beast had got somewhat rested up, we started the herd north. They were to be delivered to a man by the name of Mitchell, whose ranch was located along the Powder river, up in northern Wyoming. It was a long distance to drive cattle from Old Mexico to northern Wyoming, but to us it was nothing extraordinary as we were often called on to make even greater distances, as the railroads were not so common then as now, and transportation by rail was very little resorted to and except when beef cattle were sent to the far east, they were always transported on the hoof overland. Our route lay through southern Texas, Indian Territory, Kansas and Nebraska, to the Shoshone mountains in northern Wyoming. We had on this trip five hundred head of mostly four year old long horn steers. We did not have much trouble with them until we struck Indian Territory. On nearing the first Indian reservation, we were stopped by a large body of Indian bucks who said we could not pass through their country unless we gave them a steer for the privilege. Now as we were following the regular government trail which was a free public highway, it did not strike us as justifiable to pay our way, accordingly our boss flatly refused to give the Indians a steer, remarking that we needed all the cattle we had and proposed to keep them, but he would not mind giving them something much warmer if they interfered with us. This ultimatum of our boss had the effect of starting trouble right there. We went into camp at the edge of the Indian country. All around us was the tall blue grass of that region which in places was higher than a horse, affording an ideal hiding place for the Indians. As we expected an attack from the Indians, the boss arranged strong watches to keep a keen lookout. We had no sooner finished making camp when the Indians showed up, and charged us with a yell or rather a series of yells, I for one had got well used to the blood curdling yells of the Indians and they did not scare us in the least. We were all ready for them and after a short but sharp fight the Indians withdrew and every thing became quiet, but us cow boys were not such guys as to be fooled by the seeming quietness. We knew it was only the calm before the storm, and we prepared ourselves accordingly, but we were all dead tired and it was necessary that we secure as much rest as possible, so the low watch turned in to rest until midnight, when they were to relieve the upper watch, in whose hands the safety of the camp was placed till that time. Every man slept with his boots on and his gun near his hand. We had been sleeping several hours, but it seemed to me only a few minutes when the danger signal was given. Immediately every man was on his feet, gun in hand and ready for business. The Indians had secured reinforcements and after dividing in two bands, one band hid in the tall grass in order to pick us off and shoot us as we attempted to hold our cattle, while the other band proceeded to stampede the herd, but fortunately there were enough of us to prevent the herd from stringing out on us, as we gave our first attention to the cattle we got them to merling. Back and forward, through the tall grass, the large herd charged, the Indians being kept too busy keeping out of their way to have much time to bother with us. This kept up until daylight, but long before that time we came to the conclusion that this was the worst herd of cattle to stampede we ever struck, they seemed perfectly crazy even after the last Indian had disappeared. We were unable to account for the strange actions of the cattle until daylight, when the mystery was a mystery no longer. The Indians in large numbers had hid in the tall grass for the purpose of shooting us from ambush and being on foot they were unable to get out of the way of the herd as it stampeded through the grass, the result was that scores of the painted savages were trampled under the hoofs of the maddened cattle, and in the early gray dawn of the approaching day we witnessed a horrible sight, the Indians were all cut to pieces, their heads, limbs, trunk and blankets all being ground up in an inseparable mass, as if they had been through a sausage machine. The sight was all the more horrible as we did not know the Indians were hidden in the grass during the night, but their presence there accounted for the strange actions of the herd during the night. We suffered no loss or damage except the loss of our rest, which we sorely needed as we were all pretty well played out. However, we thought it advisable to move our herd on to a more desirable and safe camping place, not that we greatly feared any more trouble from the Indians, not soon at any rate, but only to be better prepared and in better shape to put up a fight if attacked. The second night we camped on the open plain where the grass was not so high and where the camp could be better guarded. After eating our supper and placing the usual watch the men again turned in, expecting this time to get a good night's rest. It was my turn to take the first watch and with the other boys, who were to watch with me, we took up advantageous positions on the lookout. Everything soon became still, the night was dark and sultry. It was getting along toward midnight when all at once we became aware of a roaring noise in the north like thunder, slowly growing louder as it approached, and I said to the boys that it must be a buffalo stampede. We immediately gave the alarm and started for our herd to get them out of the way of the buffalo, but we soon found that despite our utmost efforts we would be unable to get them out of the way, so we came to the conclusion to meet them with our guns and try and turn the buffalo from our direction if possible, and prevent them from going through our herd. Accordingly all hands rode to meet the oncoming stampede, pouring volley after volley into the almost solid mass of rushing beasts, but they paid no more attention to us than they would have paid to a lot of boys with pea shooters. On they came, a maddened, plunging, snorting, bellowing mass of horns and hoofs. One of our companions, a young fellow by the name of Cal Surcey, who was riding a young horse, here began to have trouble in controlling his mount and before any of us could reach him his horse bolted right in front of the herd of buffalo and in a trice the horse and rider went down and the whole herd passed over them. After the herd had passed we could only find a few scraps of poor Cal's clothing, and the horse he had been riding was reduced to the size of a jack rabbit. The buffalo went through our herd killing five head and crippling many others, and scattering them all over the plain. This was the year that the great buffalo slaughter commenced and such stampedes were common then. It seemed to me that as soon as we got out of one trouble we got into another on this trip. But we did not get discouraged, but only wondered what would happen next. We did not care much for ourselves, as we were always ready and in most cases anxious for a brush with the Indians, or for the other dangers of the trail, as they only went to relieve the dull monotony of life behind the herd. But these cattle were entrusted to our care and every one represented money, good hard cash. So we did not relish in the least having them stampeded by the Indians or run over by the buffaloes. If casualties kept up at this rate, there would not be very many cattle to deliver in Wyoming by the time we got there. After the buffalo stampede we rounded up our scattered herd and went into camp for a couple of days' rest before proceeding on our journey north. The tragic death of Cal Surcey had a very depressing effect on all of us as he was a boy well liked by us all, and it was hard to think that we could not even give him a Christian burial. We left his remains trampled into the dust of the prairie and his fate caused even the most hardened of us to shudder as we contemplated it. After getting fairly rested we proceeded on our journey north and were soon out of the Indian Territory, though we often met small bands of roving bucks, but aside from exchanging a few shots at each other they caused us no trouble. We crossed Kansas and Nebraska and reached the end of our long journey without further incident worthy of note, and we delivered our herd only five head short which was not bad considering the distance we had travelled and the events that had happened. It was a wonder that we had been able to get through with half of our herd or men. Consequently it was with genuine relief that we turned the cattle over to their new owners and received our receipt therefor. We remained at the Mitchell ranch in Wyoming several days, fraternizing with our northern brothers, swapping yarns and having a good time generally. On the return journey to Arizona we were of course, able to make better time and we returned more direct by way of Colorado and Utah, taking note of the cattle trails and the country over which we passed. In that way we secured valuable information of the trails and the country that stood us in good stead in future trips north. Arriving home at the Pete Gallinger ranch, in Arizona, we became the heroes of the range, and we received unstinted praise from our boss, but the loss of Cal Surcey was universally regretted.

We were relieved of all duty until we got thoroughly rested up, while our horses had the best the ranch afforded. But at a large cattle ranch there is always something doing and it was not long before we were again in the saddle and preparing for another trip on the trail. To the cow boy accustomed to riding long distances, life in the saddle ceases to be tiresome. It is only the dull monotony of following a large herd of cattle on the trail day after day that tires the rider and makes him long for something to turn up in the way of excitement. It does not matter what it is just so it is excitement of some kind. This the cow boy finds in dare-devil riding, shooting, roping and such sports when he is not engaged in fighting Indians or protecting his herds from the organized bands of white cattle thieves that infested the cattle country in those days. It was about this time that I hired to Bill Montgomery for a time to assist in taking a band of nine hundred head of horses to Dodge City.

The journey out was without incident, on arriving at Dodge City we sold the horses for a good price returning to the old ranch in Arizona by the way of the old lone and lonesome Dodge City trail. While en route home on this trail we had a sharp fight with the Indians. When I saw them coming I shouted to my companions, "We will battle them to hell!" Soon we heard their yells as they charged us at full speed. We met them with a hot fire from our winchesters, but as they were in such large numbers we saw that we could not stop them that way and it soon developed into a hand to hand fight. My saddle horse was shot from under me; at about the same time my partner James Holley was killed, shot through the heart. I caught Holley's horse and continued the fight until it became evident that the Indians were too much for us, then it became a question of running or being scalped. We thought it best to run as we did not think we could very well spare any hair at that particular time, any way we mostly preferred to have our hair cut in the regular way by a competent barber, not that the Indians would charge us too much, they would have probably done the job for nothing, but we didn't want to trouble them, and we did not grudge the price of a hair cut any way, so we put spurs to our horses and they soon carried us out of danger. Nearly every one of us were wounded in this fight but Holley was the only man killed on our side though a few of the Indians were made better as the result of it. We heard afterwards that Holley was scalped and his body filled with arrows by the red devils. This was only one of the many similar fights we were constantly having with the Indians and the cattle thieves of that part of the country. They were so common that it was not considered worth mentioning except when we lost a man, as on this occasion. This was the only trouble we had on this trip of any importance and we soon arrived at the Montgomery ranch in Texas where after a few days rest with the boys, resting up, I made tracks in the direction of my own crib in Arizona.

X

We Make a Trip to Nebraska. The Hole in the Wall Country. A Little Shooting Scrape. Cattle on the Trail and the Way to Handle Them. A Bit of Moralization.

The ranch boss's voice rang out sharply, but kindly as he entered our quarters where we were engaged in all sorts of occupations, some of the boys playing cards, others smoking and swapping stories, while those more industrious were diligently engaged in cleaning their forty-fives. I glanced up from my long barreled rifle I was just putting the finishing touches to, wondering what was up now. The boss informed us that we were to take another herd of cattle north, away up in the northwestern part of Nebraska, and that all of us who were on the last trip had been selected for the duty again this trip. This announcement was met with exclamations of approval from the boys who had now got thoroughly rested up and were anxious for regular duty again. Since our return from Wyoming we had not been doing much, but taking it easy with occasional range riding and were becoming rusty in consequence. We were to start on our second journey north this season as soon as possible, so we lost no time in getting ready. We were to take the same size herd as before. It did not take us long to round the herd up and the second day from the time we received the order we were off. Our route was different this time, starting from the home ranch in Arizona we went by way of New Mexico, Colorado and into Nebraska, by way of the Platte river, which we crossed near where the forks of the North and South Platte unite. It was now late in the season and we had to hurry in order to get through in good weather, therefore we put the cattle to the limit of their traveling powers. Beef cattle, that is, four year old long horns differ greatly from other cattle in their travel. The first day after being put out on the trail they will travel twenty-five miles without any trouble then as the pace begins to tell on them they fall back to fifteen or twenty miles a day, and there also seems to be an understanding among the cattle themselves that each must take a turn at leading the herd, those that start in the lead in the morning will be away back in the center of the herd at noon, and those that started in the center are now leading. This they keep up until all have had their turn at leading and as a rule if they are not scared by something they will stay pretty well bunched. We allowed the herd to graze and rest during the night, only traveling during the day, as a herd of cattle should never be moved off their grazing ground until the dew is off the grass because their feet are made soft by the wet grass and if they are moved onto the hard trail while in that condition sore heels are sure to result, and a steer with sore heels cannot travel and will have to be left behind on the trail or the herd held until those affected have recovered. Our saddle horses travel several times the distance that a herd of cattle does on the trail, as it is necessary to ride from one end of the herd to the other to keep them in line and headed in the right direction. This work is hard on the horses but that is always provided for by having a small herd of horses along under the charge of a horse rustler as we called him and any of the boys could change his tired horse for a fresh one at any time he chose, but he would have no one to help him make the change. He would have to rope, throw, saddle and bridle the horse himself without any assistance whatever from his companions, and this was no easy matter as most of the horses were wild Texas mustangs and had never had the saddle on more than once or twice and so as often happened the cow boy would be led a hard life before he finally made the change of mounts. On such occasions he always received the unwelcome and unasked advice of the other boys, but as most of the boys were expert at that business there was slight chance for railing and chaff. But if for any reason he should get the laugh from his companions he always took it in the same spirit in which it was given, only waiting his chance to get even, and such a chance was not long in coming. This particular herd acted very well and gave us no trouble to speak of. Our route lay over the old Hays' and Elsworth trail, one of the best known cattle trails in the west, then by way of Olga, Nebraska, at that time a very small and also a very tough place. It was a rendezvous of the tough element and the bad men of the cow country. There were a large number of cow boys there from the surrounding ranges and the place looked very enticing to our tired and thirsty crowd, but we had our herd to look after and deliver so we could not stop, but pushed on north crossing the Platte river, then up the trail that led by the hole in the wall country, near which place we went into camp. Then as now this hole in the wall country was the refuge of the train robbers, cattle thieves and bandits of the western country, and when we arrived the place was unusually full of them, and it was not long before trouble was brewing between our men and the natives which culminated in one of our men shooting and killing one of the bad men of the hole. Fearing more trouble and not being in the best possible shape to meet it, burdened as we were with five hundred head of cattle we broke camp at once and proceeded on our journey north. We arrived at the ranch where our herd were to be delivered without further incident and with all our cattle intact and after turning the herd over to their new owners and spending several days in getting acquainted with our northern neighbors, the Nebraska cowboys whom we found hot numbers and a jolly all round crowd of cattle men, we left for Arizona on the return journey by way of Wyoming, Colorado and New Mexico, arriving home in good shape late in the fall without further incident, and were soon engaged in range riding over our own ranges again, and getting everything in shape for the winter, but we had to be out on the range off and on all winter. Then in the spring came the usual round ups, cuttings and brandings, during which time all our men were needed at the home ranch. I had long since developed into a first class cow boy and besides being chief brand reader in Arizona and the pan handle country. My expertness in riding, roping and in the general routine of the cow boy's life, including my wide knowledge of the surrounding country, gained in many long trips with herds of cattle and horses, made my services in great demand and my wages increased accordingly. To see me now you would not recognize the bronze hardened dare devil cow boy, the slave boy who a few years ago hunted rabbits in his shirt tail on the old plantation in Tennessee, or the tenderfoot who shrank shaking all over at the sight of a band of painted Indians. I had long since felt the hot sting of the leaden bullet as it plowed its way through some portion of my anatomy. Likewise I had lost all sense of fear, and while I was not the wild blood thirsty savage and all around bad man many writers have pictured me in their romances, yet I was wild, reckless and free, afraid of nothing, that is nothing that I ever saw, with a wide knowledge of the cattle country and the cattle business and of my guns with which I was getting better acquainted with every day, and not above taking my whiskey straight or returning bullet for bullet in a scrimmage. I always had been reckless, as evidenced by my riding of Black Highwayman on the old home plantation and I never lost courage or my nerve under the most trying circumstances, always cool, observant and ready for what might turn up, made me liked and respected by my employers and those of the cattle kings of the western country it was my good fortune to meet and know.

On our own ranch, among my own companions my position was as high as a king, enjoying the trust and confidence of my employers and the homage of the men many of whom were indebted to me on occasions when my long rope or ever ready forty-five colt pistol had saved them from serious injury or death. But I thought nothing of those things then, my only ambition was to learn the business and excel in all things connected with the cow boy's life that I was leading and for which I had genuine liking. Mounted on my favorite horse, my long horsehide lariat near my hand, and my trusty guns in my belt and the broad plains stretching away for miles and miles, every foot of which I was familiar with, I felt I could defy the world. What man with the fire of life and youth and health in his veins could not rejoice in such a life? The fall and winter of 1874 passed on the Arizona ranch without any unusual occurrence, the cattle wintered well and prospects were bright for the coming year. In the early spring we again began preparing for the big round up, the brandings and the cuttings. There had been hundreds of calves and colts added to the vast herds, these all had to be cut out and branded, while all the cattle that had strayed during the winter had to be rounded up and accounted for. This work kept us in the saddle the greater part of the time. Sometimes we would be absent for days and weeks at a time on the trail of a bunch of strayed cattle. On these trips we often encountered big herds of buffalo and these supplied us with meat, and such meat! A buffalo steak fresh from a still quivering buffalo broiled over coals is a dish fit for the Gods. Coming back from one of these trips after strays early in 1875 we were notified to get ready to take a herd of five hundred head of horses up in South Dakota, the trip was a long one but horses can travel much faster than cattle and on the whole are much easier to handle. On the trails we were all happy at the prospect of the trip and were not long in getting ready and getting the horses started out on the trail, we took them by way of New Mexico, Colorado and Nebraska. They gave us very little trouble on the way up, and we reached our destination and delivered them without incident worthy of note, returning by way of Wyoming, Colorado and New Mexico. On starting out on the return journey we came down Pold creek and stopped at the old log saloon to get a drink, that being the first place where we could get any whiskey. Here in moving around among the large number of cow boys and tough characters, generally, another fuss was started between our men and some cattle rustlers resulting in some shooting, but fortunately without serious consequences.

As we were not looking for trouble, and not wishing to kill any one we left at once for home. It was our policy to always avoid trouble if possible while on these trips, but to always defend ourselves and our rights against all comers, be they white men or Indians and then it would look bad for us to have to report the loss of a man or so in a saloon fight when we were sent out to attend to business, for that reason we did not stop to give an exhibition of our fighting qualities, although we were very anxious to have matters out with them. We arrived home safely with all well and in time to assist in the round ups and the other ranch work in which we were needed.

XI

A Buffalo Hunt. I Lose My Lariat and Saddle.
I Order a Drink for Myself and My Horse. A Close
Place in Old Mexico.

When there was not much doing around the ranch, we boys would get up a buffalo hunt. Buffaloes were plentiful in those days and one did not have to ride far before striking a herd. Going out on the open plain we were not long in sighting a herd, peacefully grazing on the luxuriant grass, and it would have been an easy task to shoot them but that was not our idea of sport. In the first place it was too easy. Then to shoot them would rob the hunt of all element of danger and excitement, for that reason we prepared to rope them and then dispatch them with the knife or revolver. As soon as the herd caught sight of us they promptly proceeded to stampede and were off like the wind. We all had pretty good mounts and we started in pursuit. It is a grand sight to see a large herd of several thousand buffalo on a stampede, all running with their heads down and their tongues hanging out like a yard of red flannel, snorting and bellowing they crowd along, shaking the ground for yards around. We soon reached the rear of the herd and began operations. I had roped and dispatched several, when my attention was attracted by a magnificent bull buffalo, which I made up my mind to get, running free behind the herd. My buffalo soon came within range and my rope settled squarely over his horns and my horse braced himself for the strain but the bull proved too much for us. My horse was knocked down, the saddle snatched from under me and off my horse's back and my neck nearly broken as I struck the hardest spot in that part of Texas[.] After I got through counting the stars not to mention the moons that I could see quite plainly, I jumped to my feet and after assuring myself that I was all there I looked for my horse, he was close by just getting up while in the distance and fast growing more distant each moment was my favorite saddle flying in the breeze, hanging to the head of the infuriated buffalo.

Now I did not think I could very well lose that saddle so I sprang on my horse's bare back and started in pursuit. My horse could run like a deer and his hard fall did not seem to affect him much, so it did not take us long to overtake the plunging herd. Running my horse close up by the side of the thief who stole my saddle, I placed the muzzle of my forty-five close against his side and right there I took charge of Mr. Buffalo and my outfit.

It was no trouble to get all the buffalo meat we wanted in those days, all that was necessary was to ride out on the prairie and knock them over with a bullet, a feat that any cow boy can accomplish without useless waste of ammunition, and a running buffalo furnishes perhaps the best kind of a moving target for practice shooting. And the man that can drop his buffalo at two hundred yards the first shot can hit pretty much anything he shoots at.

I never missed anything I shot at within this distance and many a time when I thought the distance of an object was too great, the boys have encouraged me by saying, shoot, you never miss, and as much to my surprise as theirs, my old stand by placed the bullet where I aimed.

I early in my career recognized the fact that a cow boy must know how to use his guns, and therefore I never lost an opportunity to improve my shooting abilities, until I was able to hit anything within range of my forty-five or my winchester. This ability has times without number proved of incalculable value to me, when in tight places. It has often saved the life of myself and companions and so by constant practice I soon became known as the best shot in the Arizona and pan handle country.

After the buffalo hunt we were sent down in Old Mexico to get a herd of horses, that our boss had bought from the Mexicans in the southwestern part of Old Mexico. We made the journey out all right without special incident, but after we had got the horses out on the trail, headed north I was possessed with a desire to show off and I thought surprise the staid old greasers on whom we of the northern cattle country looked with contempt. So accordingly I left the boys to continue with the herd, while I made for the nearest saloon, which happened to be located in one of the low mud houses of that country, with a wide door and clay floor. As the door was standing open, and looked so inviting I did not want to go to the trouble of dismounting so urging my horse forward, I rode in the saloon, first however, scattering with a few random shots the respectable sized crowd of dirty Mexicans hanging around as I was in no humor to pay for the drinks for such a motley gathering. Riding up to the bar, I ordered keller for myself and a generous measure of pulky for my horse, both popular Mexican drinks.

NAT LOVE

The fat wobbling greaser who was behind the bar looked scared, but he proceeded to serve us with as much grace as he could command. My forty-five colt which I proceeded to reload, acting as a persuader. Hearing a commotion outside I realized that I was surrounded. The crowd of Mexican bums had not appreciated my kindly greeting as I rode up and it seems did not take kindly to being scattered by bullets. And not realizing that I could have killed them all, just as easy as I scattered them, and seeing there was but two of us—I and my horse— they had summoned sufficient courage to come back and seek revenge. There was a good sized crowd of them, every one with some kind of shooting iron, and I saw at once that they meant business. I hated to have to hurt some of them but I could see I would have to or be taken myself, and perhaps strung up to ornament a telegraph pole. This pleasant experience I had no especial wish to try, so putting spurs to my horse I dashed out of the saloon, then knocking a man over with every bullet from my Colts I cut for the open country, followed by several volleys from the angry Mexicans' pop guns.

The only harm their bullets did, however, was to wound my horse in the hip, not seriously, however, and he carried me quickly out of range. I expected to be pursued, however, as I had no doubt I had done for some of those whom I knocked over, so made straight for the Rio Grande river riding day and night until I sighted that welcome stream and on the other side I knew I was safe. Crossing the Rio Grande and entering Texas at the Eagle pass, I rode straight to the old home ranch where I stayed resting up until the boys got the horses out of Mexico into Texas, then I joined them and assisted in driving the horses into the ranch. I congratulated myself that I escaped so easily and with such little damage. It was certainly a close place but I have been in even closer places numbers of times and always managed to escape. Either through trick, the fleetness of my horse or my shooting and sometimes through all combined. At this time I was known all over the cattle country as "Red River Dick," the name given to me by the boss of the Duval outfit, when I first joined the cow boys at Dodge City, Kansas.

And many of the cattle kings of the west as well as the Indians and scores of bad men all over the western country have at some time or other had good reason to remember the name of "Red River Dick."

This was in 1875. It was not till the next year that I won the name of "Deadwood Dick," a name I made even better known than "Red River Dick." And a name I was proud to carry and defend, if necessary, with my life. This season we made several trips North. The horses we brought up from Texas now had to be driven to old man Keith's in Nebraska, on the North Platte river. On this trip we had no trouble to speak of. Several bands of Indians showed up at different times but a shot or so from one of the boys would send them scurrying off at full speed, without stopping to sample further our fighting abilities.

This was in some ways disappointing to us as we were spoiling for a fight or excitement of some kind. However, nothing turned up, so after delivering the horses to their new owners, we made tracks for home again. It was the same round of duties, season after season, but all our trips on the trail were not by any means alike, we were continually visiting new country and new scenes, traveling over trails new to us, but old in history. Many of these old trails are now famous in history.

Each trip gave us new experiences, and traveling so much as we were, there were few outfits in the cattle country that knew the trails and the country as we did. And we were continually adding to this knowledge and experience. After returning from old man Keith's in Nebraska we had to take the trail again with a herd of cattle for the Spencer brothers, whose ranch was located just north of the Red Light about sixty-five miles north of the bad lands in South Dakota. This was one of the largest cattle ranches in the West.

Their brand was known as the R Box Circle Brand There we remained for some time, adding to our knowledge of the cattle business such things as can only be learned at a large cattle ranch. On our way home we passed through Laramie, Wyoming. As fate would have it, we arrived at Laramie City on July 4, 1875, just as the notorious Jack Watkins escaped from the Albany county jail, and the excitement in the town was at fever heat. Jack Watkins, who was probably the most desperate criminal that was ever placed behind prison bars, had been arrested and placed in close confinement, as the officers of the western states had long tried to effect his capture. And they did not want to take any chances of losing him, now they had him, but for all their caution he had escaped, shooting Deputy Sheriff Lawrence in the leg, crippling him for life.

Ex-Conductor Brophy was at that time sheriff. The officers noting our arrival at such time, at once ordered us out of the city, as they suspected we knew something about the outbreak. We protested our innocence of any knowledge of the trouble. But appearances were against us, so we had to leave, going direct to Cheyenne, Wyoming.

Here we disposed of a small band of horses our boss had along, and which we did not wish to take back home with us. They were sold to the Swarn Brothers at a good price.

We remained in Cheyenne until the 18th of July, when we left for Texas, arriving at the old Pali Dora range ranch on the 10th of August. We had no more than got rested up before we were again called out on active duty. The many large cattle owners of the panhandle country had got together and come to the conclusion that the wild mustang horses, large bands of which were running wild over the Arizona and Texas plains, would make good cattle horses, and to that end a plan of campaign was arranged, whereby they could be captured, and broken in and put to some use, instead of causing damage to the range, as at present.

XII

The Big Wild Mustang Hunt. We Tire Them Out.
The Indians Capture Our Mess Wagon and Cook.
Our Bill of Fare Buffalo Meat Without Salt.

It was a bright clear morning in September as we were all gathered at the old home ranch, prepared to start on the great mustang hunt. There was one of the best men from each of the big cattle ranges in the panhandle and Arizona country, making twenty of the best range riders ever assembled together for a single purpose, while we were mounted on the best and fastest horses the Texas and Arizona cattle country could produce, while a horse rustler had left four days before with twenty more equally as good horses, giving each of us two horses apiece. We carried with us four days' rations, consisting of dried beef, crackers, potatoes, coffee—we had no sugar. The mess wagon well stocked with provisions for a two months' trip had also left four days before for a place in the wild horse district, where we knew the mustangs were to be found.

Many of the cattle men of Texas and Arizona were present to see us off, and the boss gave us a little talk on what was expected of us, and said, among other things, we were twenty of the best and gamest cow boys who ever roamed the western plains, and that he knew we would make good on hearing these words—we one and all resolved to do our best.

And swinging into the saddle we emptied our guns as a parting salutation and started on a dead run across the plains towards the scene of our duty. After a hard ride of ten days we sighted a band of about seventy-five mustangs. We at once proceeded to run them down. It was decided that twenty of us should surround the herd in a large circle, ten or fifteen miles across, which would leave a space of several miles between each rider, but not of a greater distance than he could easily cover when he saw the band coming his way or heard our signals.

The horse rustler was to keep the extra horses at a place where they would be safe and at the same time handy to the riders. Our plans completed, each rider made preparations to start for his station. But here another difficulty arose. We had not yet seen anything of our cook and mess wagon. It had not arrived at the place agreed upon, although it had had ample time to do so. Our provisions which we carried were quite low, so after waiting as long as we could, and the mess wagon failing to show up, we decided to start the hunt and take our chances on grub from what we could knock over with our guns.

Accordingly the boys all started out for their several stations. After waiting a reasonable length of time to give them an opportunity to reach their positions, we made for the herd, which as near as we could judge contained about seventy-five of the prettiest horses it was ever my pleasure to see. The magnificent stallion who happened to be on guard had no sooner seen us than he gave the danger signal to the herd, who were off like the wind, led by a beautiful snow white stallion. To get them going was our only duty at present, and we well knew the importance of saving our saddle horses for the more serious work before us. Therefore we only walked our horses, or went on a dog trot, keeping a sharp lookout for the herd's return.

The band of wild horses would run ten or fifteen miles across the prairie, where they would catch sight of the other boys, then off they would go in another direction, only to repeat the performance, as they struck the other side of the circle. In this way they would make from fifty to sixty miles to our ten, and we were slowly working them down. We kept them going this way day and night, not giving them a moment's rest or time to eat. After keeping them on the go this way for ten days we were able to get within a mile of them and could see some of the stallions taking turns at leading the herd, while other stallions would be in the rear fighting them on. In a few days more we were near enough to begin shooting the stallions out of the herd. Then we could handle them a great deal better. At this time our want of grub began to tell on us. Our cook and mess wagon had not showed up, so we had long since given them up as lost. We believed they had been captured by the Indians and future events proved we were right.

Our only food consisted of buffalo meat of which we were able to secure plenty, but buffalo meat for breakfast, dinner and supper every day without bread or salt is not the most palatable bill of fare, especially when it is all we had day after day, without any prospect of a change until we got home. But we were game and resolved to stay with our work until it was finished, especially as we only had twenty men and everyone was badly needed in the work ahead of us, so we did not think we could spare a man to return home after grub. So we swallowed our buffalo meat day after day and kept the horses moving.

They were now pretty well worked down, and we proceeded to work them toward a place where we could begin to rope them. There were now only a few stallions left in the herd as we had shot nearly all of them, and the others were too tired to cause us any trouble. We had now been out of grub over three weeks except buffalo meat and such other game as we could bring down with our guns. Our fears that the cook and mess wagon had been captured by the Indians proved well founded, as we about this time met an outfit who had seen the place where the cook was killed. They said the surroundings indicated that quite a large band had surprised the cook and driver, but that they had put up a brave fight as evidenced by the large number of empty rifle and revolver shells scattered around. Our first impulse after hearing this was to start in pursuit of the red skins and get revenge, but calmer judgment showed that such a course would be useless, because the Indians had a couple of weeks' start of us and we did not know what tribe had committed the offense as there wer so many Indians in that part of the country and in the Indian territory, and besides our horses were in no shape to chase Indians, so much to our regret our comrades had to go unrevenged at least for the present, but we all swore to make the Indians pay dearly, especially the guilty ones, if it were possible to discover who they were. We continued to work the mustangs back and forth, and in thirty days from the time we started out we had about sixty head hemmed up in Yellow Fox Canyon and were roping and riding them. They were not hard to handle as they were so poor some of them could hardly walk. This was not to be wondered at, as we had kept them on the go for the past thirty days, never once giving them a moment's rest day or night, and in that time they had very little to eat and no sleep. After roping and riding them all we got them together and headed for home.

Arriving at the ranch the mustangs were allowed to eat all they wanted and were roped and ridden until they were fairly well broken, when they were turned out with the other ranch horses. They proved good saddle horses, but as soon as they were turned out with the ranch horses they would start for their old feeding grounds, leading the other horses with them. We found it impossible to thoroughly domesticate them, so for that reason we gave them up as a bad proposition, and did not attempt to capture any more, though at that time thousands of wild mustangs were on the plains of Texas, Arizona, Wyoming and in fact all over the West. They were large, fine and as pretty a lot of horses as one could wish to see. They were seldom molested, though once in a while the Indians would make a campaign against them and capture a few, but not often, as they were so hard to capture. It was not worth the trouble, as it was almost impossible to approach them nearer than two miles, and there was always some stallions on the lookout while the others grazed over the plains, so it was out of the question to surprise them. At the first sign of danger the stallion sentinel would give his shrill neigh of warning and the herd were off like the wind.

We received unstinted praise from our employers for bringing to a successful conclusion the errand on which we were sent under such trying circumstances. But now that we were where grub was plentiful we looked on our experience as nothing to make a fuss over.

But we deeply regretted the loss of our cook and mess wagon, and we resolved that if we ever found the guilty parties to make it rather warm for them. This we never did, neither did we ever hear more of the fate of the cook. Our work, so far as trips on the trail were concerned, was over for this season, and we could count on a long rest until spring, as aside from range riding and feeding there was nothing doing around the home ranch. But sometimes the range riding kept us on the go pretty lively, especially during and after a big storm, which sometimes scattered the cattle all over the surrounding country, and it would take some lively riding to get them all together again. Then the Indians and the white cattle thieves would make raids on our herds, running them off in great numbers and stampeding the balance of the herd.

This generally resulted in us chasing them sometimes for miles over the prairies, and we generally were successful in recovering our cattle and punishing the cattle thieves in a manner that they did not soon forget. But then again sometimes they would stampede the herd in the night, and under the cover of darkness and the excitement would manage to make off with some of the best horses or the choicest cattle, and by the time we missed them the thieves would have such a start that it was impossible to overtake them, but if they were overtaken, vengeance was swift and sure.

XIII

In the spring of 1876 orders were received at the home ranch for three thousand head of three-year-old steers to be delivered near Deadwood, South Dakota. This being one of the largest orders we had ever received at one time, every man around the ranch was placed on his mettle to execute the order in record time.

Cow boys mounted on swift horses were dispatched to the farthest limits of the ranch with orders to round up and run in all the three-year-olds on the place, and it was not long before the ranch corrals began to fill up with the long horns as they were driven by the several parties of cow boys; as fast as they came in we would cut out, under the bosses' orders such cattle as were to make up our herd.

In the course of three days we had our herd ready for the trail and we made our preparations to start on our long journey north. Our route lay through New Mexico, Colorado and Wyoming, and as we had heard rumors that the Indians were on the war path and were kicking up something of a rumpus in Wyoming, Indian Territory and Kansas, we expected trouble before we again had the pleasure of sitting around our fire at the home ranch. Quite a large party was selected for this trip owing to the size of the herd and the possibility of trouble on the trail from the Indians. We, as usual, were all well armed and had as mounts the best horses our ranch produced, and in taking the trail we were perfectly confident that we could take care of our herd and ourselves through anything we were liable to meet. We had not been on the trail long before we met other outfits, who told us that General Custer was out after the Indians and that a big fight was expected when the Seventh U.S. Cavalry, General Custer's command, met the Crow tribe and other Indians under the leadership of Sitting Bull, Rain-in-the-Face, Old Chief Joseph, and other chiefs of lesser prominence, who had for a long time been terrorizing the settlers of that section and defying the Government.

As we proceeded on our journey it became evident to us that we were only a short distance behind the soldiers. When finally the Indians and soldiers met in the memorable battle or rather massacre in the Little Big Horn Basin on the Little Big Horn River in northern Wyoming, we were only two days behind them, or within 60 miles, but we did not know that at the time or we would have gone to Custer's assistance. We did not know of the fight or the outcome until several days after it was over. It was freely claimed at the time by cattle men who were in a position to know and with whom I talked that if Reno had gone to Custer's aid as he promised to do, Custer would not have lost his entire command and his life.

It was claimed Reno did not obey his orders, however that may be, it was one of the most bloody massacres in the history of this country. We went on our way to Deadwood with our herd, where we arrived on the 3rd of July, 1876, eight days after the Custer massacre took place.

The Custer Battle was June 25, '76, the battle commenced on Sunday afternoon and lasted about two hours. That was the last of General Custer and his Seventh Cavalry. How I know this so well is because we had orders from one of the Government scouts to go in camp, that if we went any farther North we were liable to be captured by the Indians.

We arrived in Deadwood in good condition without having had any trouble with the Indians on the way up. We turned our cattle over to their new owners at once, then proceeded to take in the town. The next morning, July 4th, the gamblers and mining men made up a purse of $200 for a roping contest between the cow boys that were then in town, and as it was a holiday nearly all the cow boys for miles around were assembled there that day. It did not take long to arrange the details for the contest and contestants, six of them being colored cow boys, including myself. Our trail boss was chosen to pick out the mustangs from a herd of wild horses just off the range, and he picked out twelve of the most wild and vicious horses that he could find.

The conditions of the contest were that each of us who were mounted was to rope, throw, tie, bridle and saddle and mount the particular horse picked for us in the shortest time possible. The man accomplishing the feat in the quickest time to be declared the winner.

It seems to me that the horse chosen for me was the most vicious of the lot. Everything being in readiness, the "45" cracked and we all sprang forward together, each of us making for our particular mustang.

I roped, threw, tied, bridled, saddled and mounted my mustang in exactly nine minutes from the crack of the gun. The time of the next nearest competitor was twelve minutes and thirty seconds. This gave me the record and championship of the West, which I held up to the time I quit the business in 1890, and my record has never been beaten. It is worthy of passing remark that I never had a horse pitch with me so much as that mustang, but I never stopped sticking my spurs in him and using my quirt on his flanks until I proved his master. Right there the assembled crowd named me Deadwood Dick and proclaimed me champion roper of the western cattle country.

The roping contest over, a dispute arose over the shooting question with the result that a contest was arranged for the afternoon, as there happened to be some of the best shots with rifle and revolver in the West present that day. Among them were Stormy Jim, who claimed the championship; Powder Horn Bill, who had the reputation of never missing what he shot at; also White Head, a half breed, who generally hit what he shot at, and many other men who knew how to handle a rifle or 45-colt.

The range was measured off 100 and 250 yards for the rifle and 150 for the Colt 45. At this distance a bulls eye about the size of an apple was put up. Each man was to have 14 shots at each range with the rifle and 12 shots with the Colts 45.

I placed every one of my 14 shots with the rifle in the bulls eye with ease, all shots being made from the hip; but with the 45 Colts I missed it twice, only placing 10 shots in the small circle. Stormy Jim being my nearest competitor, only placing 8 bullets in the bulls eye clear, the rest being quite close, while with the 45 he placed 5 bullets in the charmed circle. This gave me the championship of rifle and revolver shooting as well as the roping contest, and for that day I was the hero of Deadwood, and the purse of $200 which I had won on the roping contest went toward keeping things moving, and they did move as only a large crowd of cattle men can move things. This lasted for several days when most of the cattle men had to return to their respective ranches, as it was the busy season, accordingly our outfit began to make preparations to return to Arizona.

In the meantime news had reached us of the Custer massacre, and the indignation and sorrow was universal, as General Custer was personally known to a large number of the cattle men of the West. But we could do nothing now, as the Indians were out in such strong force.

There was nothing to do but let Uncle Sam revenge the loss of the General and his brave command, but it is safe to say not one of us would have hesitated a moment in taking the trail in pursuit of the blood thirsty red skins had the opportunity offered.

Everything now being in readiness with us we took the trail homeward bound, and left Deadwood in a blaze of glory. On our way home we visited the Custer battle field in the Little Big Horn Basin.

There was ample evidence of the desperate and bloody fight that had taken place a few days before. We arrived home in Arizona in a short time without further incident, except that on the way back we met and talked with many of the famous Government scouts of that region, among them Buffalo Bill (William F. Cody), Yellow Stone Kelley, and many others of that day, some of whom are now living, while others lost their lives in the line of duty, and a finer or braver body of men never lived than these scouts of the West. It was my pleasure to meet Buffalo Bill often in the early 70s, and he was as fine a man as one could wish to meet, kind, generous, true and brave.

Buffalo Bill got his name from the fact that in the early days he was engaged in hunting buffalo for their hides and furnishing U.P. Railroad graders with meat, hence the name Buffalo Bill. Buffalo Bill, Yellowstone Kelley, with many others were at this time serving under Gen. C. C. Miles.

The name of Deadwood Dick was given to me by the people of Deadwood, South Dakota, July 4, 1876, after I had proven myself worthy to carry it, and after I had defeated all comers in riding, roping, and shooting, and I have always carried the name with honor since that time.

We arrived at the home ranch again on our return from the trip to Deadwood about the middle of September, it taking us a little over two months to make the return journey, as we stopped in Cheyenne for several days and at other places, where we always found a hearty welcome, especially so on this trip, as the news had preceded us, and I received enough attention to have given me the big head, but my head had constantly refused to get enlarged again ever since the time I sampled the demijohn in the sweet corn patch at home.

Arriving at home, we received a send off from our boss and our comrades of the home ranch, every man of whom on hearing the news turned loose his voice and his artillery in a grand demonstration in my honor.

But they said it was no surprise to them, as they had long known of my ability with the rope, rifle and 45 Colt, but just the same it was gratifying to know I had defeated the best men of the West, and brought the record home to the home ranch in Arizona. After a good rest we proceeded to ride the range again, getting our herds in good condition for the winter now at hand.

XIV

RIDING THE RANGE. THE FIGHT WITH YELLOW DOG'S TRIBE. I AM
CAPTURED AND ADOPTED BY THE INDIANS. MY ESCAPE. I RIDE
A HUNDRED MILES IN TWELVE HOURS WITHOUT A SADDLE. MY
INDIAN PONY. "YELLOW DOG CHIEF." THE BOYS PRESENT ME WITH
A NEW OUTFIT. IN THE SADDLE AND ON THE TRAIL AGAIN.

It was a bright, clear fall day, October 4, 1876, that quite a large
number of us boys started out over the range hunting strays which
had been lost for some time. We had scattered over the range and I
was riding along alone when all at once I heard the well known Indian
war whoop and noticed not far away a large party of Indians making
straight for me. They were all well mounted and they were in full war
paint, which showed me that they were on the war path, and as I was
alone and had no wish to be scalped by them I decided to run for it. So
I headed for Yellow Horse Canyon and gave my horse the rein, but as I
had considerable objection to being chased by a lot of painted savages
without some remonstrance, I turned in my saddle every once in a while
and gave them a shot by way of greeting, and I had the satisfaction of
seeing a painted brave tumble from his horse and go rolling in the dust
every time my rifle spoke, and the Indians were by no means idle all this
time, as their bullets were singing around me rather lively, one of them
passing through my thigh, but it did not amount to much. Reaching
Yellow Horse Canyon, I had about decided to stop and make a stand
when one of their bullets caught me in the leg, passing clear through it
and then through my horse, killing him. Quickly falling behind him I
used his dead body for a breast work and stood the Indians off for a long
time, as my aim was so deadly and they had lost so many that they were
careful to keep out of range.

But finally my ammunition gave out, and the Indians were quick to
find this out, and they at once closed in on me, but I was by no means
subdued, wounded as I was and almost out of my head, and I fought
with my empty gun until finally overpowered. When I came to my
senses I was in the Indians' camp.

My wounds had been dressed with some kind of herbs, the wound
in my breast just over the heart was covered thickly with herbs and
bound up. My nose had been nearly cut off, also one of my fingers

had been nearly cut off. These wounds I received when I was fighting my captors with my empty gun. What caused them to spare my life I cannot tell, but it was I think partly because I had proved myself a brave man, and all savages admire a brave man and when they captured a man whose fighting powers were out of the ordinary they generally kept him if possible as he was needed in the tribe.

Then again Yellow Dog's tribe was composed largely of half breeds, and there was a large percentage of colored blood in the tribe, and as I was a colored man they wanted to keep me, as they thought I was too good a man to die. Be that as it may, they dressed my wounds and gave me plenty to eat, but the only grub they had was buffalo meat which they cooked over a fire of buffalo chips, but of this I had all I wanted to eat. For the first two days after my capture they kept me tied hand and foot. At the end of that time they untied my feet, but kept my hands tied for a couple of days longer, when I was given my freedom, but was always closely watched by members of the tribe. Three days after my capture my ears were pierced and I was adopted into the tribe. The operation of piercing my ears was quite painful, in the method used, as they had a small bone secured from a deer's leg, a small thin bone, rounded at the end and as sharp as a needle. This they used to make the holes, then strings made from the tendons of a deer were inserted in place of thread, of which the Indians had none. Then horn ear rings were placed in my ears and the same kind of salve made from herbs which they placed on my wounds was placed on my ears and they soon healed.

The bullet holes in my leg and breast also healed in a surprisingly short time. That was good salve all right. As soon as I was well enough I took part in the Indian dances. One kind or another was in progress all the time. The war dance and the medicine dance seemed the most popular. When in the war dance the savages danced around me in a circle, making gestures, chanting, with every now and then a blood curdling yell, always keeping time to a sort of music provided by stretching buffalo skins tightly over a hoop.

When I was well enough I joined the dances, and I think I soon made a good dancer. The medicine dance varies from the war dance only that in the medicine dance the Indians danced around a boiling pot, the pot being filled with roots and water and they dance around it while it boils. The medicine dance occurs about daylight.

I very soon learned their ways and to understand them, though our conversation was mostly carried on by means of signs. They soon gave me to understand that I was to marry the chief's daughter, promising me 100 ponies to do so, and she was literally thrown in my arms; as for the lady she seemed perfectly willing if not anxious to become my bride. She was a beautiful woman, or rather girl; in fact all the squaws of this tribe were good looking, out of the ordinary, but I had other notions just then and did not want to get married under such circumstances, but for prudence sake I seemed to enter into their plans, but at the same time keeping a sharp lookout for a chance to escape. I noted where the Indians kept their horses at night, even picking out the handsome and fleet Indian pony which I meant to use should opportunity occur, and I seemed to fall in with the Indians' plans and seemed to them so contented that they gave me more and more freedom and relaxed the strict watch they had kept on me, and finally in about thirty days from the time of my capture my opportunity arrived.

My wounds were now nearly well, and gave me no trouble. It was a dark, cloudy night, and the Indians, grown careless in their fancied security, had relaxed their watchfulness. After they had all thrown themselves on the ground and the quiet of the camp proclaimed them all asleep I got up and crawling on my hands and knees, using the greatest caution for fear of making a noise, I crawled about 250 yards to where the horses were picketed, and going to the Indian pony I had already picked out I slipped the skin thong in his mouth which the Indians use for a bridle, one which I had secured and carried in my shirt for some time for this particular purpose, then springing to his back I made for the open prairie in the direction of the home ranch in Texas, one hundred miles away. All that night I rode as fast as my horse could carry me and the next morning, twelve hours after I left the Indians camp I was safe on the home ranch again. And my joy was without bounds, and such a reception as I received from the boys. They said they were just one day late, and if it hadn't been for a fight they had with some of the same tribe, they would have been to my relief. As it was they did not expect to ever see me again alive. But that they know that if the Indians did not kill me, and gave me only half a chance I would get away from them, but now that I was safe home again, nothing mattered much and nothing was too good for me.

It was a mystery to them how I managed to escape death with such wounds as I had received, the marks of which I will carry to my grave and it is as much a mystery to me as the bullet that struck me in the breast just over the heart passed clear through, coming out my back just below the shoulder. Likewise the bullet in my leg passed clear through, then through my horse, killing him.

Those Indians are certainly wonderful doctors, and then I am naturally tough as I carry the marks of fourteen bullet wounds on different part of my body, most any one of which would be sufficient to kill an ordinary man, but I am not even crippled. It seems to me that if ever a man bore a charm I am the man, as I have had five horses shot from under me and killed, have fought Indians and Mexicans in all sorts of situations, and have been in more tight places than I can number. Yet I have always managed to escape with only the mark of a bullet or knife as a reminder. The fight with the Yellow Dog's tribe is probably the closest call I ever had, and as close a call as I ever want.

The fleet Indian pony which carried me to safety on that memorable hundred mile ride, I kept for about five years. I named him "The Yellow Dog Chief." And he lived on the best the ranch afforded, until his death which occurred in 1881, never having anything to do except an occasional race, as he could run like a deer. I thought too much of him to use him on the trail and he was the especial pet of every one on the home ranch, and for miles around.

I heard afterwards that the Indians persued me that night for quite a distance, but I had too much the start and besides I had the fastest horse the Indians owned. I have never since met any of my captors of that time. As they knew better than to venture in our neighborhood again. My wound healed nicely, thanks to the good attention the Indians gave me. My captors took everything of value I had on me when captured. My rifle which I especially prized for old associations sake; also my forty fives, saddle and bridle, in fact my whole outfit leaving me only the few clothes I had on at the time.

My comrades did not propose to let this bother me long, however, because they all chipped in and bought me a new outfit, including the best rifle and revolvers that could be secured, and I had my pick of the ranch horses for another mount. During my short stay with the Indians I learned a great deal about them, their ways of living, sports, dances, and mode of warfare which proved of great benefit to me in after years. The oblong shields they carried were made from tanned buffalo skins and so tough were they made that an arrow would not pierce them although I have seen them shoot an arrow clean through a buffalo. Neither will a bullet pierce them unless the ball hits the shield square on, otherwise it glances off.

All of them were exceedingly expert with the bow and arrow, and they are proud of their skill and are always practicing in an effort to excel each other. This rivalry extends even to the children who are seldom without their bows and arrows.

They named me Buffalo Papoose, and we managed to make our wants known by means of signs. As I was not with them a sufficient length of time to learn their language, I learned from them that I had killed five of their number and wounded three while they were chasing me and in the subsequent fight with my empty gun. The wounded men were hit in many places, but they were brought around all right, the same as I was. After my escape and after I arrived home it was some time before I was again called to active duty, as the boys would not hear of me doing anything resembling work, until I was thoroughly well and rested up. But I soon began to long for my saddle and the range.

And when orders were received at the ranch for 2000 head of cattle, to be delivered at Dodge City, Kansas, I insisted on taking the trail again. It was not with any sense of pride or in bravado that I recount here the fate of the men who have fallen at my hand.

It is a terrible thing to kill a man no matter what the cause. But as I am writing a true history of my life, I cannot leave these facts out. But every man who died at my hands was either seeking my life or died in open warfare, when it was a case of killing of being killed.

XV

On a Trip to Dodge City, Kan. I Rope One of Uncle Sam's
Cannon. Captured by the Soldiers. Bat Masterson to
My Rescue. Lost on the Prairie. The Buffalo Hunter Cater.
My Horse Gets Away and Leaves Me Alone on the Prairie.
The Blizzard. Frozen Stiff.

In the spring of 1877, now fully recovered from the effects of the very serious wounds I had received at the hands of the Indians and feeling my old self again, I joined the boys in their first trip of the season, with a herd of cattle for Dodge City. The trip was uneventful until we reached our destination. This was the first time I had been in Dodge City since I had won the name of "Deadwood Dick", and many of the boys, who knew me when I first joined the cow boys there in 1869, were there to greet me now. After our herd had been delivered to their new owners, we started out to properly celebrate the event, and for a space of several days we kept the old town on the jump.

And so when we finally started for home all of us had more or less of the bad whiskey of Dodge City under our belts and were feeling rather spirited and ready for anything.

I probably had more of the bad whiskey of Dodge City than any one and was in consequence feeling very reckless, but we had about exhausted our resources of amusement in the town, and so were looking for trouble on the trail home.

On our way back to Texas, our way led past old Fort Dodge. Seeing the soldiers and the cannon in the fort, a bright idea struck me, but a fool one just the same. It was no less than a desire to rope one of the cannons. It seemed to me that it would be a good thing to rope a cannon and take it back to Texas with us to fight Indians with.

The bad whiskey which I carried under my belt was responsible for the fool idea, and gave me the nerve to attempt to execute the idea. Getting my lariat rope ready I rode to a position just opposite the gate of the fort, which was standing open. Before the gate paced a sentry with his gun on his shoulder and his white gloves showing up clean and white against the dusty grey surroundings. I waited until the sentry had passed the gate, then putting spurs to my horse I dashed straight for and through the gate into the yard. The surprised sentry called halt, but I paid no attention to him. Making for the cannon at full speed my rope left my hand and settled square over the cannon, then turning and putting spurs to my horse I tried to drag the cannon after me, but strain as he might my horse was unable to budge it an inch. In the meantime the surprised sentry at the gate had given the alarm and now I heard the bugle sound, boots and saddles, and glancing around I saw the soldiers mounting to come after me, and finding I could not move the cannon, I rode close up to it and got my lariat off then made for the gate again at full speed. The guard jumped in front of me with his gun up, calling halt, but I went by him like a shot, expecting to hear the crack of his musket, but for some reason he failed to fire on me, and I made for the open prairie with the cavalry in hot pursuit.

My horse could run like a wild deer, but he was no match for the big, strong, fresh horses of the soldiers and they soon had me. Relieving me of my arms they placed me in the guard house where the commanding officer came to see me. He asked me who I was and what I was after at the fort. I told him and then he asked me if I knew anyone in the city. I told him I knew Bat Masterson. He ordered two guards to take me to the city to see Masterson. As soon as Masterson saw me he asked me what the trouble was, and before I could answer, the guards told him I rode into the fort and roped one of the cannons and tried to pull it out. Bat asked me what I wanted with a cannon and what I intended doing with it. I told him I wanted to take it back to Texas with me to fight the Indians with; then they all laughed. Then Bat told them that I was all right, the only trouble being that I had too much bad whiskey under my shirt. They said I would have to set the drinks for the house. They came to $15.00, and when I started to pay for them, Bat said for me to keep my money that he would pay for them himself, which he did. Bat said that I was the only cowboy that he liked, and that his brother Jim also thought very much of me. I was then let go and I joined the boys and we continued on our way home, where we arrived safely on the 1st of June, 1877.

We at once began preparing for the coming big round up. As usual this kept us very busy during the months of July and August, and as we received no more orders for cattle this season, we did not have to take the trail again, but after the round up was over, we were kept busy in range riding, and the general all around work of the big cattle ranch. We had at this time on the ranch upwards of 30,000 head of cattle, our own cattle, not to mention the cattle belonging to the many other interests without the Pan Handle country, and as all these immense herds used the range of the country, in common as there was no fences to divide the ranches, consequently the cattle belonging to the different herds often got mixed up and large numbers of them strayed.

At the round ups it was our duty to cut out and brand the young calves, take a census of our stock, and then after the round up was over we would start out to look for possible strays. Over the range we would ride through canyons and gorges, and every place where it was possible for cattle to stray, as it was important to get them with the main herd before winter set in, as if left out in small bunches there was danger of them perishing in the frequent hard storms of the winter. While range riding or hunting for strays, we always carried with us on our saddle the branding irons of our respective ranches, and whenever we ran across a calf that had not been branded we had to rope the calf, tie it, then a fire was made of buffalo chips, the only fuel besides grass to be found on the prairie.

The irons were heated and the calf was branded with the brand of the finder, no matter who it personally belonged to.

It now became the property of the finder. The lost cattle were then driven to the main herd. After they were once gotten together it was our duty to keep them together during the winter and early spring. It was while out hunting strays that I, got lost, the first and only time I was ever lost in my life, and for four days I had an experience that few men ever went through and lived, as it was a close pull for me.

I had been out for several days looking for lost cattle and becoming separated from the other boys and being in a part of the country unfamiliar to me. It was stormy when I started out from the home ranch and when I had ridden about a hundred miles from home it began to storm in earnest, rain, hail, sleet, and the clouds seemed to touch the earth and gather in their inpenterable embrace every thing thereon. For a long time I rode on in the direction of home, but as I could not see fifty yards ahead it was a case of going it blind. After riding for many weary hours through the storm I came across a little log cabin on the Palidore river. I rode up to within one hundred yards of it where I was motioned to stop by an old long haired man who stepped out of the cabin door with a long buffalo gun on his arm. It was with this he had motioned me to stop.

I promptly pulled up and raised my hat, which, according to the custom of the cowboy country, gave him to understand I was a cowboy from the western cow ranges. He then motioned me to come on. Riding up to the cabin he asked me to dismount and we shook hands.

He said, when I saw you coming I said to myself that must be a lost cowboy from some of the western cow ranges. I told him I was lost all right, and I told him who I was and where from. Again we shook hands, he saying as we did so, that we were friends until we met again, and he hoped forever. He then told me to picket out my horse and come in and have some supper, which very welcome invitation I accepted.

His cabin was constructed of rough hewn logs, somewhat after the fashion of a Spanish block house. One part of it was constructed under ground, a sort of dug out, while the upper portion of the cabin proper was provided with many loop holes, commanding every direction.

He later told me these loop holes had stood him in handy many a time when he had been attacked by Indians, in their efforts to capture him. On entering his cabin I was amazed to see the walls covered with all kinds of skins, horns, and antlers. Buffalo skins in great numbers covered the floor and bed, while the walls were completely hidden behind the skins of every animal of that region, including large number of rattle snakes skins and many of their rattles.

His bed, which was in one corner of the dug out, was of skins, and to me, weary from my long ride through the storm, seemed to be the most comfortable place on the globe just then. He soon set before me a bountious supper, consisting of buffalo meat and corn dodgers, and seldom before have I enjoyed a meal as I did that one. During supper he told me many of his experiences in the western country. His name was Cater, and he was one of the oldest buffalo hunters in that part of Texas, having hunted and trapped over the wild country ever since the early thirties, and during that time he had many a thrilling adventure with Indians and wild animals.

I stayed with him that night and slept soundly on a comfortable bed he made for me. The next morning he gave me a good breakfast and I prepared to take my departure as the storm had somewhat moderated, and I was anxious to get home, as the boys knowing I was out would be looking for me if I did not show up in a reasonable time.

My kind host told me to go directly northwest and I would strike the Calones flats, a place with which I was perfectly familiar. He said it was about 75 miles from his place. Once there I would have no difficulty in finding my way home. Cater put me up a good lunch to last me on my way, and with many expressions of gratitude to him, I left him with his skins and comfortable, though solitary life. All that day and part of the night I rode in the direction he told me, until about 11 o'clock when I became so tired I decided to go into camp and give my tired horse a rest and a chance to eat. Accordingly I dismounted and removed the saddle and bridle from my horse I hobbled him and turned him loose to graze on the luxuriant grass, while I, tired out, laid down with my head on my saddle fully dressed as I was, not even removing my belt containing my 45 pistol from my waist, laying my Winchester close by. The rain had ceased to fall, but it was still cloudy and threatening. It was my intention to rest a few hours then continue on my way; and as I could not see the stars on account of the clouds and as it was important that I keep my direction northwest in order to strike the Flats, I had carefully taken my direction before sundown, and now on moving my saddle I placed it on the ground pointing in the direction I was going when I stopped so that it would enable me to keep my direction when I again started out. I had been laying there for some time and my horse was quietly grazing about 20 yards off, when I suddenly heard something squeal. It sounded like a woman's voice. It frightened my horse and he ran for me. I jumped to my feet with my Winchester in my hand. This caused my horse to rear and wheel and I heard his hobbles break with a sharp snap. Then I heard the sound of his galloping feet going across the Pan Handle plains until the sound was lost in the distance. Then I slowly began to realize that I was left alone on the plains on foot, how many miles from home I did not know. Remembering I had my guns all right, it was my impulse to go in pursuit of my horse as I thought I could eventually catch him after he had got over his scare, but when I thought of my 40 pound saddle, and I did not want to leave that, so saying to myself that is the second saddle I ever owned, the other having been taken by the Indians when I was captured, and this saddle was part of the outfit presented to me by the boys, and so tired and as hungry as a hawk, I shouldered my saddle and started out in the direction I was going when I went into camp, saying to myself as I did so, if my horse could pack me and my outfit day and night I can at least pack my outfit. Keeping my direction as well as I could I started out over the prairie through the dark, walking all that night and all the next day without anything to eat or drink until just about sundown and when I had begun to think I would have to spend another night on the prairie without food or drink, when I emerged from a little draw on to a raise on the prairie, then looking over on to a small flat I saw a large herd of buffalo. These were the first I had seen since I became lost and the sight of them put renewed life and hope in me as I was then nearly famished, and when I saw them I knew I had something to eat.

Off to one side about 20 yards from the main herd and about 150 yards from me was a young calf. Placing my Winchester to my shoulder I glanced along the shining barrel, but my hands shook so much I lowered it again, not that I was afraid of missing it as I knew I was a dead shot at that distance, but my weakness caused by my long enforced fast and my great thirst made my eyes dim and my hands shake in a way they had never done before, so waiting a few moments I again placed the gun to my shoulder and this time it spoke and the calf dropped where it had stood. Picking up my outfit I went down to where my supper was laying. I took out my jack knife and commenced on one of his hind quarters. I began to skin and eat to my hearts content, but I was so very thirsty. I had heard of people drinking blood to quench their thirst and that gave me an idea, so cutting the calf's throat with my knife I eagerly drank the fresh warm blood.

It tasted very much like warm sweet milk. It quenched my thirst and made me feel strong, when I had eaten all I could, I cut off two large chunks of the meat and tied them to my saddle, then again shouldering the whole thing I started on my way feeling almost as satisfied as if I had my horse with me. I was lost two days, and two nights, after my horse left me and all that time I kept walking packing my 40 pounds saddle and my Winchester and two cattle pistols.

On the second night about daylight the weather became more threatening and I saw in the distance a long column which looked like smoke. It seemed to be coming towards me at the rate of a mile a minute. It did not take it long to reach me, and when it did I struggled on for a few yards but it was no use, tired as I was from packing my heavy outfit for more than 48 hours and my long tramp, I had not the strength to fight against the storm so I had to come alone. When I again came to myself I was covered up head and foot in the snow, in the camp of some of my comrades from the ranch.

It seemed from what I was told afterwards that the boys knowing I was out in the storm and failing to show up, they had started out to look for me, they had gone in camp during the storm and when the blizzard had passed they noticed an object out on the prairie in the snow, with one hand frozen, clenched around my Winchester and the other around the horn of my saddle, and they had hard work to get my hands loose, they picked me up and placed me on one of the horses and took me to camp where they stripped me of my clothes and wrapped me up in the snow, all the skin came off my nose and mouth and my hands and feet had been so badly frozen that the nails all came off. After [I] had got thawed out in the mess wagon and took me home in 15 days I was again in the saddle ready for business but I will never forget those few days I was lost and the marks of that storm I will carry with me always.

XIV

The Old Haze and Elsworth Trail. Our Trip to Cheyenne.
Ex-Sheriff Pat A. Garret. The Death of "Billy the Kid".
The Lincoln County Cattle War.

Early the next spring 1878 we went on a short trip to Junction City,
Kan., with a small herd of horses for Hokin and Herst. We started
out from the home ranch early in April, stringing the herd out along
the old Haze and Elsworth trail. Everything went well until we were
several days out and we had went in camp for the night. The herd had
been rounded up and were grazing in the open prairie under the usual
watch. And all the cowboys except the first watch had turned in for
a good night's rest, when it began to storm finally developing into a
genuine old fashioned Texas storm, with the usual result that the herd
stampeded.

The watch at once gave the alarm and we awoke to find everything
in confusion. It was a very dark night and under such circumstances it is
hard to control a herd of horses in a stampede. In a few moments every
man was in the saddle, as we always kept our saddle horse picketed out,
so they could not join the other horses. And it was our custom when on
the trail with a herd of horses on going into camp to leave our saddle
horses, saddled and bridled, merely loosing the cinches of the saddles
though sometimes we removed the bridles, to enable them to graze
better. So when the alarm was given in this instance, it did not take
us long to get in the saddle and after the horses who were now going
across the prairie as only frightened horses can go in a stampede.

The storm continued with more or less fury all night and it was late
the next day before we got the herd rounded up and under any sort
of control. The next morning we found that one of the boys, Frank
Smith, had lost his horse and outfit during the night. While chasing
the horses over the prairie, his horse stepped in a prairie dog's hole and
fell. Throwing his rider and snatching the rope out of Smith's hand,
the horse made off over the prairie carrying with him bridle, saddle
and outfit, and we never saw or heard of him again. After getting our
breakfast, we continued north, and all went well with us until we struck
the Wakeeny river, near Junction City, when in fording the stream. It
was high water and we were forced to swim our horses across. All went

well with the herd and the boys were following when one of them came near being drowned, and was only saved by my quick rope.

I had entered the river and my horse was swimming easily, when on glancing around I saw one of the boys, Loyd Hoedin by name, go under the water. Both man and horse completely disappeared. They soon came up only to disappear again. I saw at once something was wrong so when they came up the second time I threw my rope. It fell near Hoedin, who had the presence of mind to grasp it, and hold on while I snaked both man and horse out to safety. After reaching Junction City and turning the herd over to their new owners we started out to have the usual good time. This lasted for several days during which time we cleaned up pretty near all the money there was in the Junction with our horses in a six hundred yard race, between ourselves and cow boys from different outfits who happened to be in the city.

Our horses without exception proved the fastest runners, accordingly we pocketed considerable coin, and in consequence we were feeling first rate when we struck the trail homeward bound. We arrived at the home ranch all right in June. This was the last trip we were called to make this season, and our time for the remainder of the year was taken up with the general routine work of the large cattle ranch.

Late the next season we took the trail en route to Cheyenne, Wyoming, with two thousand head of fine Texas steers for the Swan Brothers, 20 mlies northwest of Cheyenne. Nothing of unusual importance happened on this trip aside from the regular incidents pertaining to driving such a large herd of cattle on the trail. We had a few stampedes and lost a few cattle, arriving in Cheyenne we had a royal good time for a few days as usual before starting home. On arriving at the home ranch again we found considerable excitement, owing to the war between the cattle men and cattle rustlers and every man was needed at home and few there were who did not take part in one way or another in the most bitter and furious cattle war of history and I being one of the leading cowboys of the West, necessarily took an active part in the dispute and many were the sharp clashes between the waring factions that I witnessed and fought in and was wounded many times in these engagements. For years the cattle rustlers had been invading the large cattle ranges belonging to the large cattle kings of the West and running off and branding large numbers of choice cattle and horses, this led to many a sharp fight between the cowboys and the rustlers, but of late these thieves had become so bold and the losses of the cattle men had become so great that the latter determined to put a stop to it, and so open war was declared.

On one side was the large ranchmen and cattle men and on the other the Indians, half breeds, Mexicans and white outlaws that made the cattle country their rendezvous. The cattle men had now organized with the given determination of either killing or running out of the country for good these thieves, who had caused them so much loss. And during the war many of them cashed in and the others for the most part left for pastures new, having been virtually whipped out of the country. It was a desperate and bloody war while it lasted.

But it was satisfactory to the cattle men who could now rest easier in the security of their herds and their grazing grounds. It was at this time that I saw considerable of William H. Bonney alias "Billie the kid", the most noted desperado and all around bad man the world has known.

The first time I met Billie the Kid was in Antonshico, New Mexico, in a saloon, when he asked me to drink with him, that was in 1877. Later he hired to Pete Galligan, the man in whose employ I was. Galligan hired the Kid to drive his buck board between the White Oaks, the nearest town, and Galligan's ranch with provisions for the boys, and the Kid told me himself that one [of] these trips he would drive the team, on a dead run, the whole distance of 30 miles to the Oaks in order to get there quick so he would have more time to stay around town before it was time to start back, then when he would arrive home the team was nearly dead from exhaustion. He remained in the employ of Galligan for about eleven months, then he was hired by John Chisholm to rustle cattle for him. Chisholm agreed to pay the Kid so much per head for all the cattle the Kid rustled. When the time came for a settlement, Chisholm failed to settle right or to the Kid's saisfaction, then the Kid told Chisholm he would give him one day to make up his mind to settle right, but before the Kid could see Chisholm again, Chisholm left the country going east where his brother was. The Kid then swore vengence, and said he would take his revenge out of Chisholm's men, and he at once began killing all the employ of John Chisholm. He would ride up to a bunch of cowboys and enquire if they worked for Chisholm. If they replied in the affirmative, he would shoot them dead on the spot, and few men were quicker with a 45 or a deadly shot than "Billie the Kid". The next time I met the Kid was in Holbrook, Arizona, just after a big round up. The Kid, Buck Cannon, and Billie Woods were together. I was on my way to Silver City, New Mexico, in the fall of 1880 when I met them, and as they were going there also, we rode on together[.] The "Kid" showed me the little log cabin where he said he was born. I went in the cabin with him, and he showed me how it was arranged when he lived there, showing me where the bed sat and the stove and table. He then pointed out the old postoffice which he said he had been in lots of times.

He told me he was born and raised in Silver City, New Mexico, which is near the Moggocilion Mountains, and at that time the Kid was badly wanted by the sheriffs of several counties for numerous murders committed by him mostly of John Chisholm's men in Texas and New Mexico.

The Kid bid me good bye. He said he was going to the mountains as he knew them well, and once there he was all right as he could stand off a regiment of soldiers. The three of them departed together. I never saw him again until the spring of 1881. I was in the city of Elmorgo, New Mexico, and saw him the morning he was forced to flee to the mountains to escape arrest. We could see him up there behind the rocks. He was well armed having with him two Winchesters and two 45 Colts revolvers and plenty of ammunition, and although the officers wanted him badly, no one dared go up after him as it was certain death to come with range of the Kid's guns. Later on he escaped and the next time I saw him was in Antonshico, New Mexico. It was in June, and we had come up from Colonas after some saddle horses, and I met and talked with him.

The next time I saw him he was laying dead at Pete Maxwell's ranch in Lincoln county, New Mexico, having been killed by Pat A. Garret at that time sheriff of Lincoln county, New Mexico. We arrived in Lincoln county the very night he was killed at Pete Maxwell's ranch and went into camp a short distance from Maxwell's, and we saw the Kid a short time after he had been killed. The Kid had been arrested by Pat Garret and his posse a short time before at Stinking Springs, New Mexico, along with Tom Pickett, Billy Wilson and Dave Rudebough, after arresting these men which was only effected after a hard fight and after the Kid's ammunition had given out. Garret took the men heavily ironed to Los Vegas. When it became known that Billy the Kid had been captured a mob formed for the purpose of lynching him. But Garret placed his prisoners in a box car over which himself and deputies stood guard until the train pulled out which was nearly two hours. During that time the mob was furious to get at the men, but they well knew the temper of Sheriff Garret so they kept their distance.

The men were tried and convicted. The Kid and Rudbough were sentenced to be hanged. Rudbough for having killed a jailer at Los Vegas in 1880. The judge on passing sentence on the Kid, said you are sentenced to be hanged by the neck until you are dead-dead-dead. The Kid laughed in the judge's face saying, and you can go to Hell, Hell, Hell. After the Kid had been sentenced he was placed in jail at Los Vegas, ironed hand and foot, and under heavy guard, but never lost confidence and was always looking for a chance to escape. When the day of his execution was not much more than a week off, the Kid saw his chance, while eating his supper both handcuffs had been fastened to one wrist so the Kid could better feed himself. He was only guarded by one deputy named Bell. The other deputy, Ollinger, had gone to supper across the street from the jail. Bell turned his head for a moment and the Kid noticing the movement quick as a flash brought the handcuffs down on Bell's head, stunning him. The Kid then snatched Bell's revolver, he shot the deputy through the body. Bell staggered to the steps down which he fell and into the yard below where he died. Ollinger hearing the shot rushed across the street. As he entered the jail yard he looked up and saw the Kid at a window. As he did so the Kid shot Ollinger dead with a shot gun which was loaded with buck shot. The Kid then broke the gun across the window sill, then going to the room where the weapons were kept the Kid picked out what guns he wanted and broke the balance. Then he made the first person he met break the irons from his legs and bring him a horse. The Kid then took four revolvers and two Winchester rifles and rode away. Sheriff Garret was at White Oaks at the time and as soon he as heard of the escape he hurried home and organized a posse to recapture the Kid, but the Kid was at liberty two months before he was finally rounded up and killed at Pete Maxwell's ranch. At the time the Kid escaped at Los Vegas myself and a party of our boys had our horses at Menderhall and Hunter's livery stable, just a few doors from the jail and I was standing on the street talking to a friend when the Kid rode by. From Los Vegas he went to the borders of Lincoln county where his ever ready revolver was always in evidence. Shortly after his escape he shot and killed William Mathews and a companion whom he met on the prairie without apparent cause, and several other murders were attributed to him before he was finally located at Maxwell's ranch and killed by Sheriff Garret.

The Kid was only 22 years of age when his wild career was ended by the bullet from the sheriff's gun and it is safe to assert he had at lease one murder to the credit of every year of his life. He was killed by Sheriff Garret in a room of one of the old houses at Fort Sumner, known at that time as Maxwell's ranch, July 12, 1881, about two months after his escape from the Lincoln county jail, and Sheriff Pat A. Garret, one of the nervest men of that country of nervy men and the only man who ever pursued the Kid and lived to tell the tale, is at present at the head of the Customs Service at El Paso, Texas, and to meet him and note his pleasant smile and kindly disposition, one would not believe him the man who sent Billie the Kid to his last account. But behind the pleasant twinkle in his eye and the warm hand clasp there is a head as cool and a nerve as steady as ever held a 45.

XVII

ANOTHER TRIP TO OLD MEXICO. I ROPE AN ENGINE.
I FALL IN LOVE. MY COURTSHIP. DEATH OF MY SWEETHEART.
MY PROMISED WIFE. I MUST BEAR A CHARMED LIFE.
THE ADVENT OF PROGRESS. THE LAST OF THE RANGE.

On one of these memorable trips after cattle, and with cattle on the trail, one that I will most likely remember, the longest was a trip to Old Mexico after a herd of horses. It was on this trip that I fell in love, the first time in my life. During my wild career on the western plains I had met many handsome women, and they often made much of me, but somehow I had never experienced the feeling called love, until I met my charming sweetheart in Old Mexico. I had perhaps been too much absorbed in the wild life of the plains, in the horses, and cattle which made up my world, to have the time or inclination to seek or enjoy the company of the gentler sex. But now that I had met my fate, I suppose I became as silly about it as any tenderfoot from the east could possibly be, as evidence of how badly I was hit. While on the trail with the herd our route lay along a narrow gauge railroad, and I was feeling up in the air caused no doubt partly from the effects of love and partly from the effects of Mexican whiskey, a generous measure I had under my belt, however I was feeling fine, so when the little engine came puffing along in the distance I said to the boys I have roped nearly everything that could be roped, so now I am going to rope the engine. They tried to persuade me not to make the attempt, but I was in no mood to listen to reason or anything else, so when the engine came along I put my spurs to my horse and when near enough I let fly my lariat. The rope settled gracefully around the smoke stack, and as usual my trained horse set himself back for the shock, but the engine set both myself and my horse in the ditch, and might have continued to set us in places had not something given way, as it was the rope parted, but the boys said afterwards that they thought they would have to send for a wrecking train to clean the track or rather the ditch.

Roping a live engine is by long odds worse than roping wild Buffalo on the plains or Uncle Sam's cannon at the forts. This incident cleared the atmosphere somewhat, but my love was as strong as ever and I thanked my lucky start she did not see me as they dragged me out of the ditch.

I first saw my sweetheart as we were driving the herd along the dusty road, passing a small adobe house near the city of Old Mexico. I saw a handsome young Spanish girl standing in the yard and I suppose I fell in love with her at first sight, anyway I pretended to be very thirsty and rode up and asked her for a drink. She gave it to me and I exchanged a few words with her before joining the boys and the herds.

After that I saw her quite often during my stay in Old Mexico before we again returned home. One day shortly before I was to leave for the North I went to see her and overheard a conversation between her and her mother, in which her mother said to her: "My daughter will you leave your mother for to go with the wild cowboy?" And she answered no mother I will not leave you to go with any wild cowboy. On hearing this I bid her goodbye and a long farewell, as I told her I did not expect to ever see her again. Then leaping to the back of my faithful horse I rode like mad across the Mexican plains, until I had somewhat cooled down, but it was a hard blow to me, as I truly loved her. After that I joined the boys and returned up the trail with them. Six or seven months later we were again in Old Mexico with a herd of cattle and went in camp some distance out from the city, and as soon as she heard our outfit had returned she rode out to the camp and after looking around and not seeing me, she said to the camp boss, "Where is the wild cowboy that was here with you last time? Did he not come up the trail with you". The boss told her I had come up the trail but that I had not been seen since crossing the last mountains as of course he knew whom she meant as my little love affair was pretty generally known among the boys. When the boss told her that I had not been seen since they had crossed the last mountains, she hung her head and looked completely heart broken. I was lying in the mess wagon at the time an interested spectator of all that took place, and seeing her looking so downhearted I could hardly restrain myself from jumping out of the wagon and taking her in my arms. After a time she slowly raised her head and looked long and wistfully up the trail. Then turning to the camp boss again she said, "Camp boss tell me truly if Nat Love works with you and did he come on this trip with you". The boss answered her as before that I had not been seen since crossing the last mountains, which was true as I had been riding in the mess wagon. On hearing the boss' answer she took it as final and started to ride away.

I thought it high time to make my presence known, as with the sight of her, all my old love returned, and I forgot every thing except that I loved her. So I jumped out of the wagon exclaiming here I am, and in a minute we were locked in each others arms and I believe I kissed her before all the boys, but I didn't care, she was mine now. We became engaged and were to be married in the fall and were to make our home in the city of Mexico, but in the spring she took sick and died. Her death broke me all up and after I buried her I became very wild and reckless, not caring what happened to me and when you saw me in the saddle you saw me at home, and while I saw many women since I could never care for any as I did for her. And I vainly tried to forget her and my sorrow in the wild life of the plains and every danger I could find courting death in fights with Indians and Mexicans and dare devil riding on the range, but it seemed to me that I bore a charmed life. Horses were shot from under me, men were killed around me, but always I escaped with a trifling wound at the worst. As time passed I began to recover from my disappointment and to take my old interest in the work of the ranch, and as my reputation had spread over the country I did not lack work, but was kept on the go all the time, first with one large cattle owner, then with another. Most of my working being in the round ups and brandings, brand reading, and with large herds on the trail, as during my long experience in the cattle country I had traveled every known trail, and over immense stretches of country where there was no sign of a trail, nothing but the wide expanse of prairie; bare except for the buffalo grass, with here and there a lone tree or a giant cactus standing as a lone sentinel in the wildest of long stretches of grazing land rolling away in billows of hill and gully, like the waves of the ocean. Likewise I could read, identify and place every brand or mark placed on a horse or steer between the Gulf of Mexico and the borders of Canada, on the North and from Missouri to California. Over this stretch of country I have often traveled with herds of horses or cattle or in searching for strays or hunting the noble buffalo on his own native feeding grounds. The great buffalo slaughter commenced in the west in 1874, and in 1877 they had become so scarce that it was a rare occasion when you came across a herd containing more than fifty animals where before you could find thousands in a herd. Many things were responsible for the slaughter, but the principal reason that they had now become so scarce was that in 1875 and 1876 the Indians started to kill them in large numbers for their skins. Thousands were killed by them, skinned and the carcasses left as food for the wolves and vultures of the prairie. Many were killed by the white hunters to furnish meat for the railroad graders and the troups at the frontier forts.

While the big cattle ranches were always kept well supplied with buffalo meat, on the stock of my rifle is one hundred and twenty-six notches, each one representing a fine buffalo that has fallen to my own hand, while some I have killed with the knife and 45 colts, I forgot to cut a notch for. Buffalo hunting, a sport for kings, thy time has passed. Where once they roamed by the thousands now rises the chimney and the spire, while across their once peaceful path now thunders the iron horse, awakening the echoes far and near with bell and whistle, where once could only be heard the sharp crack of the rifle or the long doleful yelp of the coyote. At the present time the only buffalo to be found are in the private parks of a few men who are preserving them for pleasure or profit.

With the march of progress came the railroad and no longer were we called upon to follow the long horned steers, or mustangs on the trail, while the immense cattle ranges, stretching away in the distance as far as the eye could see, now began to be dotted with cities and towns and the cattle industry which once held a monopoly in the west, now had to give way to the industry of the farm and the mill. To us wild cowboys of the range, used to the wild and unrestricted life of the boundless plains, the new order of things did not appeal, and many of us became disgusted and quit the wild life for the pursuits of our more civilized brother. I was among that number and in 1890 I bid farewell to the life which I had followed for over twenty years.

It was with genuine regret that I left the long horn Texas cattle and the wild mustangs of the range, but the life had in a great measure lost its attractions and so I decided to quit it and try something else for a while. During my life so far I had no chance to secure an education, except the education of the plains and the cattle business. In this I recognize no superior being. Gifted with a splendid memory and quick observation I learned and remembered things that others passed by and forgot, and I have yet to meet the man who can give me instruction in the phases of a life in which I spent so long. After quitting the cowboy life I struck out for Denver. Here I met and married the present Mrs. Love, my second love. We were married August 22, 1889, and she is with me now a true and faithful partner, and says she is not one bit jealous of my first love, who lies buried in the city of Old Mexico.

One year later, in 1890, I accepted a position in the Pullman service on the Denver and Rio Grande Railroad, running between Denver and Salida, Colorado. The Pullman service was then in its infancy, so to speak, as there was as much difference between the Pullman sleeping cars of those days and the present as there is between the ox team and the automobile.

XVIII

After my marriage in Denver, I rented a small cottage which I comfortably furnished and we, Mrs. Love and myself, started to housekeeping in a modest way. Then I began to look around for a job, but to a man who was used to the excitement and continual action of the range and the cattle ranches, the civilized and quiet life of the city is apt to prove stale and uninteresting. It was that way with me, and after passing up several jobs offered to me I thought I would try railroading for awhile, probably for the same reason that prompted me to leave home twenty years before; I still wanted to see the world. With that idea in mind, I went to the Pullman offices in Denver, and after making some inquiries I was directed to the office of Superintendent Rummels who was at that time superintendent of the Pullman service.

A Mr. Wright was his assistant. I found Superintendent Rummels in his office, and I asked him if he wanted to hire any more porters. He asked me if I had ever worked for the Pullman company. I told him no that I had been a cowboy ever since I was 16 years old. He then asked me if I had money enough to buy my pullman uniform. I asked him how much it would cost and he said $22.00. I told him yes, I had the price. He asked me if I knew any one in Denver. I told him yes and gave him the name of Mr. Sprangler who had my money in his bank. Supt. Rummels told me to get a letter from Mr. Sprangler and he would put me on. So I went and got the letter and with it the money to pay for my uniform, after having my measure taken and sending for my suit. I borrowed a uniform from one of the other porters and the second day after I called on the superintendent I was sent on the run between Denver and Salida. One of the old men put me on to my duties and showed me how to make up my car and the general run of things.

On my first trip I found a kind friend in the Pullman conductor, a Mr. Keely, who helped me in many ways and I suppose I made many blunders as the difference between a Pullman car and the back of a

Texas mustang is very great. However I managed to get around among the passengers in my car, and attend to their needs in some sort of a way.

My first trouble commenced when I succeeded in getting the shoes of passengers which had been given to me to polish, badly mixed up. The shoes of a portly red faced man whose berth was in the forward end of the car, I placed by the berth of a tall and slim western yankee at the other end of the car, while a number 7 and a number 9 shoe were placed decorously by the berth of a sour spinster from New York. This naturally caused a good sized rumpus the next morning. And sundry blessings were heaped on the head of yours truly. Nearly all the passengers were mad and the tips were conspicuous by their absence. That made me mad and thoroughly disgusted with the job. On returning to Denver I again called on Superintendent Rummels and told him that I had enough of the Pullman service, and would rather go back to the cattle and the range. Superintendent Rummels tried to persuade me to stay with it saying I had done all right, and would improve with experience but I was thoroughly disgusted and wanted no more of it, so I turned in my keys, got my uniform and walked out. So again I was without a job.

After going around Denver for several days, it struck me that there was money to be made selling fruit, vegetables, honey and chickens around the town. Accordingly I purchased a horse and wagon and an assorted stock and started out on my new vocation. This proved profitable from the start and I made good money which caused me to stay with it for nearly a year, when my natural restfulness caused me to become discontented and to yearn for more excitement and something a little faster so I disposed of my stock, horse and wagon, and started out to look for something else to do, but that something else was about as hard to find as the proverbial needle in the straw stack, at that particular time. Whether it was fate or the talk of the other porters whom I met I finally concluded to give the Pullman service another try. Accordingly I called on Mr. J. M. Smith who was now district superintendent of the Pullman service and asked him for a job. He asked me if I had been in the company's service before and I told him yes. He asked me how long and I told him one trip, and I told him why I quit, and that the tips were too slow for me. He asked me if I thought it was any better now, and I said I did not know whether it was any better or not but that I thought I could do better.

He told me the whole secret of success was in pleasing all my passengers. I told him I thought it was all right about pleasing two or three passengers but when it came to pleasing a whole car full of passengers, that was another matter. He said to try anyway. He than assigned me to a car running on the narrow gauge line between Denver and Alamosa, Creed and Durango. This was the real beginning of my Pullman service.

I ran on the Colorado roads under Superintendent Smith for a number of years and always found him courteous and obliging, always ready and willing to help us with advice and counsel, but what proved a mystery to me for a long time was how the superintendent managed to find out things that happened on my car when he was not present. Sometimes when I went to report or met him he would question me about things that happened on my run, such as pleasing the passengers and other things, which I did not suppose he knew a thing about and inquiries among the other trainmen only deepened the mystery.

I would ask the Pullman conductor if he told the superintendent such and such a thing and he would say no. Then I would ask him how the superintendent knew about them as he was not on the train. He would say he did not know. This kept up until finally I made up my mind that if there ever was a clairvoyant the superintendent certainly was one.

The fact that he was able to find out things that happened hundreds of miles away without any one telling him, kept me worked up for a long time until I finally tumbled to the special agents who are employed to travel as common passengers and report how things are going to the superintendent. That explained the whole mystery, but it did not in any way make me move easy in my mind, because if a special agent was along one trip, there was no reason to think that one was not along every trip. At least I made up my mind there was, and governed myself accordingly, but the increased attention given to my passengers as a result caused an increase in the tips, that came my way. With the increase in my earnings and the experience I was gaining I came to have a liking for the service, which is in no wise diminished at this time. I soon learned the knack of pleasing the greater number of my passengers, and this reported to the superintendent by the special agents raised me in the official's favor with the result that I was given more extensive and more profitable runs and soon became one of the most popular porters in Colorado. This brought with it increased responsibilities as well as increased profits and favors enjoyed.

When I started to work it was for $15.00 per month this has been increased from time to time until at present owing to my long service and having gained a thorough knowledge of my business, I am often made porter in charge. This position pays me as high as $40.00 per month. The difference between a porter and a porter in charge is that a porter generally has a car over which a Pullman conductor presides, which the porter in charge owing to his long service and his knowledge of the business is placed in full charge of a car, making the services of a Pullman conductor unnecessary. A porter in the employ of the Pullman company for ten years and giving good service for that time receives from the company two suits of clothes per year, and other privileges not enjoyed by the beginner.

A porter just beginning in the service has to purchase his own uniform, the cost of which is never less than $20.00 for the summer suit or $22.00 for the winter suit. After five years of good service a porter is entitled to wear one white stripe on his coat sleeve to which one is added for every succeeding five years of good service. Naturally the porter that understands his business and gives his whole attention to the passengers in his car and to his work, will make more money than the porter who has not the patience to try and please his passengers. I have had porters complain to me about the small amount they were able to earn in the service and on questioning them I found it was wholly because they did not think it necessary to try and make friends of the people in their car. I early recognized the fact that if I expected to succeed in the Pullman service I must make all the friends I could on my runs, and the cases are very rare where I have failed to receive a tip of some kind from my passengers, although as it happens sometimes I have people in my car who are not very well blessed with this world's goods, and who can ill afford to spend money in tips. To such people I always give the same attention and care, as if I was sure to receive a $10 tip, and they rarely failed to give me a kind thank you, on leaving my car. In the course of our duties we naturally meet all manner of people, the business man out for business or pleasure, the drummers who nearly always give us a tip; the wife going to join her sick husband or the husband hurrying home to the bedside of his sick child; the invalid in search of health, or the family going home to attend the funeral of a loved one; the young man going to be married, and the young couple on their honeymoon; the capitalist, the miner, the sportsman and the vast army of people that go to make up the traveling public, who like the sands of the desert are forever shifting around from place to place, and with whom we porters are brought in closer contact perhaps than any one else on their travels. We must necessarily be good judges of human nature to be able to please the majority of the people who travel under our care. We nearly always receive a tip from those who ride with us for any distance. The size of the tip often depends on the mode of the passenger giving it. Even those who ride with us only a short distance often give us a tip of more generous proportions than will the man who has ridden with us several thousands of miles. The superintendent himself when he rides in our car, we are sure to receive from him 25 cents or 50 cents for a day or a day's ride.

The smallest tip I have received from a passenger during my service was 2 cents. This amount I received from a rather cranky individual, who when I went to brush him off handed me two copper cents and followed them up with the remark that some of us porters needed calling down and some needed knocking down. My opinion if what he needed caused me to smile, wherein he wanted to know what I was smiling at. Needless to say I did not feel like wasting any more breath on him so I bundled his boxes and satchel out on the platform and left him to follow at his leisure.

The largest tips I ever received from a single traveler was $25.00 given me by one of the Rothschilds whom I brought from Chicago to Frisco, but this has been largely surpassed several times in car tips or trips. The Knights Templar one of whose cars I had charge of between Denver and Boston made, up a purse of $150.00 and presented it to me with the compliments of the passengers in recognition of the good service I had rendered them. While in charge of the private car of General Manager Fisher in a trip through California and Mexico, Mr. Fisher made up a purse of $75.00 for me, in recognition of my attentions to the members of his party. But the man who gave me 5 cents received as much attention from me as the man who gives me $5.00. It is perhaps all he can afford and the manner in which he gives it often makes up for the smallness of the tip.

XIX

The Pullman Sleeping Car. Long Trips on the Rail.
The Wreck. One Touch of Nature Makes the Whole
World Kin. A Few of the Railroads Over Which
I have Traveled. The Invalid and
the Care We Give Them.

The modern Pullman sleeping car is a veritable palace on wheels furnished in the best materials, without regard to expense, comfort, convenience and the safety of the passengers being the main object. To say that the builders of the Pullman cars have succeeded in attaining this object is but a mild expression. Fine carpets cover the floors, the seats and chairs are upholstered in the best and softest of material, while every convenience is provided for the use of the lucky mortal who is called across the continent on business or pleasure, and whose pleasure it is to travel and sleep in the Pullman sleeping car of the present day. The traveler of today when he has to go from Chicago to San Francisco, simply throws a few things in a grip, is driven to the Union terminal station in Chicago, where he secures a through ticket and a sleeping car berth. At the car steps he is met by the Pullman porter who relieves him of his grip and assists him on the train if necessary. From that time until four days later when he arrives in San Francisco, he has no more care. If he wishes to write letters there is a handy writing tablet with stationery and everything needful. He can write his letters and hand them to the porter to mail and continue his perusal of the morning paper. If he gets hungry he has but to step in the dining car, where he will find viands fit for a king. If he wants a shave or a haircut, the barber is in the next car. If he wants to view the scenery en route, the observation car is but a few steps away. When he gets sleepy and wishes to retire he presses the electric button at his elbow and the porter will do the rest, but if he prefers to lay in his luxurious bed and read, he has but to turn on the electric light at his bedside and he can read as long as he pleases, and when he arrives at San Francisco he will be cleanly shaven, nicely brushed, with his shoes freshly shined, and on the outside of a good breakfast, ready to tackle at once the business or the pleasure that brought him across the continent. Or, if the traveler prefers, he may swing aboard the magnificently equipped and royally appointed Los Angeles Limited, one of the finest through trains that this mundane sphere can boast. Catch this train in Chicago, which you may do any day in the year, and it will carry you with safety, speed and comfort over the fertile farms, meadows and plains; through the City of the Saints on the second day; then around the Great Dead Sea of America, over the sage brush plains and grazing ranges of southern Nevada, and into the Land of Sunshine and Flowers and the City of the Angels on the third day after leaving your home in Chicago.

What a contrast to the mode of travel our grandfathers were forced to adopt, a decade ago, when the old ox team and the prairie schooner wended its slow way over the mountains and plains, over trails in every turn of which lurked danger and death. "Verily the sun do move." During my service with the Pullman company I have traveled from the Atlantic to the Pacific and from the Gulf of Mexico to the borders of Canada, over nearly all the many different lines of railroad that makes the map of North America look like a spider had been crawling over it in search of a fly. I have visited all the principal cities and towns where the sound of the bell and the whistle is heard, and I have in a great measure satisfied my desire to see the country. Among the great lines of railway over which I have traveled are the Union Pacific, whose overland limited, the Atlantic Express and the Portland-Chicago Special, are the acme of quick, safe and comfortable travel. The overland limited is electric lighted, steam heated and contains every known luxury and convenience of travel. The Denver and Rio Grande Railroad is noted the world over for its quick time, fine scenery, comfort and safety. The Southern Pacific, the Baltimore & Ohio Southwestern, the Missouri Pacific between St. Louis and all points east, all electric lighted trains with observation, parlor, cafe dining cars and Pullman sleeping cars; the Chicago & Northwestern, whose through train service to Chicago and the East from San Francisco, Los Angeles, Portland, Salt Lake, Ogden and Denver is not excelled in any land; the Illinois Central Railroad, whose eight track entrance to Chicago from the south along the lake front is one of the triumphs of Yankee railroading, and whose train service is elegant in the extreme. The Pennsylvania lines which will take you from Chicago to New York in eighteen hours and make you feel thoroughly comfortable while doing it. The Louisville and Nashville Railroad, whose lines reach every town and hamlet in the solid South. The Nickel Plate road, the direct line from Chicago to New York, Boston and all points east, all trains of the Nickel Plate road arrive and depart from the new LaSalle Street station, one of the finest railroad stations in the country. The Santa Fe, from whose trains you can view some of the finest scenery in the Rocky Mountains, including the Grand Canyon of Arizona, a mile deep, thirteen miles wide, two hundred and seventeen miles long and painted like a flower. The Lehigh Valley Railroad to Chicago, New York and Philadelphia, from whose car windows one may view the world-famous Niagara Falls. The Colorado & Southern, the Colorado road over which travel is one continuous delight. The San Pedro, Los Angeles and Salt Lake Railroad, one of the youngest but by no means the least of railroads, the road that lies as straight as the crow flies, linking together the City of the "Saints" and the City of the "Angels." The snow-capped Rocky Mountains and the sun-kissed shores of the Pacific Ocean, the dead sea and the live sea; the railroad that makes it possible to have a sleigh ride with your second wife in the City of the "Saints" on Sunday and pick flowers and eat oranges with your first wife in the City of the "Angels" on Tuesday. Over this line I am running at present, and while it has only been in operation a short time, yet the time and service equals and in some cases surpasses the time and service of the great Trunk Lines of the east. We often make ninety miles an hour over the standard gauge roadbed, that equals any in this country. The cars are all new, the engines are the latest up-to-date kind. The cars are built for comfort and convenience, the trains are all electric lighted, steam heated and have every modern convenience for the safety and comfort of the passengers. This road, in common with some of the eastern roads employs chair car porters in addition to the Pullman porters. On all trains from Salt Lake to Los Angeles there are three or four Pullman porters and one chair car porter.

All trains have dining cars, which are in reality magnificent dining rooms, where three times a day the dainties of the season are prepared by a competent chef to satisfy the most discriminating inner man. The furnishings of these cars, the fine linen, the artistic glass (china and silverware, are guaranteed to make you enjoy your meal, even if you have got dyspepsia. Besides the dining car and the Pullman sleeping cars, there is attached to all overland trains on the Salt Lake route, a through tourist sleeper, which differs from the Pullman sleeper only in a slight difference in the furnishings. The service is the same, but the cost of a berth in them between Salt Lake and Los Angeles is just one-half that of the standard sleeepr. I have never run on a road where better service, more courteous treatment or better time was made than on the S. P., L. A. & S. L. Railroad.

In these latter years, when progress is the watchword of the railroads in common with the other industries of the country, no expense or pains are spared by the railroad people to add to the comfort, enjoyments, safety and convenience of the traveling public, until now it is about as safe to travel as it is to stay at home, and not much if any more expensive. But in spite of all safeguards adopted by the railroads a wreck occurs once in a while the same as accidents occur at home.

The first wreck I was in the train struck a split switch with the result that the cars turned over and piled up in a ditch. That happened in Colorado. We were forced to crawl out through the windows, like a prairie dog out of his hole. No one was killed but the passengers were all pretty well shaken up and somewhat scared. As soon as the cars got comfortably piled up and the passengers were able to speak they all commenced yelling for the porter. But at that particular moment the porter was busy rubbing his shins and assuring himself there was nothing to be scared about. The passengers at such times are apt to forget that the porter is as scared as they are, and has forgotten all about tips and such commonplace matters as that, but after he gets his wits about him he loses no time in looking after his flock, and rendering assistance to such of his passengers as need it, and most of them do need assistance of some kind if for no other reason than to be assured that they are not hurt. The Pullman porter of today must be a very versatile sort of a person, he must have plenty of patience, be a good judge of human nature, quick, kind and observant. Many are the times a gouty and crusty passenger has traveled in my car, who was in such a bad humor that it was next to impossible to please him, yet before he had ridden a hundred miles with me, I had him in good humor and laughing with the rest of the passengers. "Laugh and the whole world laughs with you."

It is by no means an uncommon thing for us porters to be called upon to turn nurse for sick or invalid passengers in our car, and often have I watched by the bedside of a sick passenger, feeding him, giving him medicine, bathing him and in fact becoming for the time being a

NAT LOVE

hospital nurse, and many are the blessings I have received from my sick passengers, both men and women, whose pain I have eased, and their last moments on earth I have cheered. And this, dear reader, we do in the name of humanity and not in the name of tips.

XX

The Tourist Sleeping Car. The Chair Car.
The Safeguards of Modern Railroading. See America,
Then Let Your Chest Swell with Pride that
You are an American.

The Pullman tourist sleeping car, which you can find on all through trains of the different railroads throughout the United States, are to the traveler of moderate means what the Pullman car is to the millionaire traveler. They are designed for the comfort and convenience of the traveling public to whom the expenditure of a dollar more or less is a matter of moment, and who cannot afford or do not care for the small extra show and tinsel of the Pullman sleeping car, but whose only desire is to make their journey pleasant, comfortable and safe. This they can do as well in the tourist as in the standard sleeping car.

There is a difference in price that will amount to a tidy sum in a long trip across the continent, but that fact does not always appeal to the traveling public, as I have had the poorest of passengers in the palace car and at other times a millionaire and his family would be my passengers in the tourist cars. It seems to me a matter of fact and one which my long experience seems to verify, that the American traveler does not care so much about his comfort as his ability to get there, as the average American traveler is always in a hurry and in nine cases out of ten, he is thinking more about the speed of the train than he is about his immediate surroundings or the price he had paid for his ticket. The railroads, knowing this, have made and are continually making every effort to add to the speed and safety of their trains, but traveling long distances is a tiresome matter at the best and for that reason the railroads are continually making improvements with a view to add to the comfort, convenience and pleasure of the traveler, and in a journey such as one from Chicago to Los Angeles, for instance, there is no time to stop for meals and such trivial matters as a shave, as time is money lost to most of the passengers and to the railroad company also. For that reason the sleeping car is provided that you may sleep with as much comfort as if you were in your own home, the dining car is provided to furnish you a good meal on the fly and at a price that all can afford. The library and drawing room cars are provided, where you can make yourself as comfortable as you can in your own house. The porter will get your morning paper, furnish you with writing materials or your morning high ball, and look after you like a hen after her brood.

But on all railroads there are rules governing the passengers as well as the employees, the same as there are in all lines of business. A passenger may not, for instance, smoke in the body of the Pullman car, but must retire to the drawing room or his stateroom. As an instance in point, I had J. J. Corbett for a passenger in my car between Ogden and Chicago, a gentleman who was at that time in the height of his career and naturally thought he owned the earth or a large part of it, at any rate he came in the sleeper from the dining car, lit a cigar, propped his feet upon the opposite seat and prepared for a comfortable smoke. But it was against the rules to smoke in that part of the car, so I approached him and politely requested him not to smoke in that part of the car. He regarded me a few moments and with a sneer said, "So you are Mr. Pullman, are you?" I told him I was not Mr. Pullman, but I was in charge of one of Mr. Pullman's cars, and for that reason I was a representative of Mr. Pullman, and that it was strictly against the rules to smoke in that part of the car, and that if he wished to smoke he would have to go to the drawing room. He went, but the sleeping car conductor, who had watched the incident, told me I had better look out or Corbett would have my scalp. I told the conductor I was not scared and that if Corbett hadn't gotten out I would have thrown him out, all of which I meant, but the conductor shook his head and said to look out. Sure enough the matter was reported to the superintendent, but that official on hearing the facts in the matter said I had done perfectly right, and what I was paid to do.

It is necessary that all passengers as well as all employees shall observe the rules of the company, for the benefit, safety and enjoyment of all the passengers and employees alike.

All the railroad men I have met from the president down have all proved themselves jolly good fellows, kind, considerate and always ready to render assistance and service to those in need, but at the same time they are strict about the rules and discipline. Thoroughly understanding their business themselves, they insist on the beginner obeying instructions and the laws of the road, because on that depends on the lives of hundreds of people, and the value of thousands of dollars worth of property, and for the same reason they are expending thousands of dollars annually in new appliances, inventions and equipment, that will add to the saving of time or insure the safety of the traveler. Among the new inventions adopted by the modern railroads are the "Block" System, which makes collisions between two trains approaching each other on the same track almost an impossibility if the engineer is awake and attentive to business. Under this system when the trains approach a certain distance of each other a bell is rung in the cab of each locomotive simultaneously, and will continue to ring until the danger is over. This with the powerful electric headlights now used, with which the roadbed is lit up for a distance of five miles, makes a head-on collision almost impossible, while the air brakes, heavy rails, solid roadbed, doing away with the sharp curves and heavy grades, all add to the safety of the passengers and the saving of many miles in travel and many precious moments. It has always seemed strange to me that so many Americans rush off to Europe and foreign countries every year in search of health and pleasure, or to climb the Alps in Switzerland, and to view the scenery of the old world, when our own North America, the new world, offers so many better opportunities to study Dame Nature in all her phases, and I always say to the traveling American, "See America." How many of you have done so? Only those who have seen this grand country of ours can justly appreciate the grandeur of our mountains and rivers, valley and plain, canyon and gorge, lakes and springs, cities and towns, the grand evidences of God's handiwork scattered all over this fair land over which waves the stars and stripes. Go to New York and view the tall buildings, the Brooklyn bridge, the subway, study the works of art to be found there, both in statuary and painting, ponder on the vast volume of commerce carried on with the outside world. Note the many different styles of architecture displayed in the palace of the millionaire and the house of the humble tradesman, view the magnificent Hudson river and the country homes along its grassy, tree-lined shores, note the ships from every clime riding at anchor in the East river. Then speculate on the changes that have been wrought in the course of the short time since Manhattan Island was purchased from the Indians by Pete Minuts for a few blankets and beads amounting in value to $24.00. Then board the Pennsylvania Limited, whose trains are the acme of modern railroading and go to Washington, the nation's capital city. Walk along Pennsylvania avenue and note its beauty. Visit the capitol and let your chest swell out with pride that you are an American. Visit the tomb of General Grant and the thousand and one magnificent statues scattered throughout the city. Visit Annapolis and West Point, where the leaders of the nation's navy and army are trained. Walk over the battlefields of Fredricksburg, Gettysburg and Lexington, and let your mind speculate on the events that made modern history.

Note the majestic Potomac and the Washington monument. Take a short trip north and see the great Niagara Falls, listen to what they tell you in their mighty roaring voice. Go to Pittsburg where the great steel works are located, and see how the steel pen and the steel cannon are made. Go to Chicago, that western hive of commerce. See the Great Lakes, or better still take a cruise on them. Note the great lumber industry of Michigan, and the traffic of the lakes. Go to Kansas City and Omaha and see the transformation of the Texas steer into the corned beef you ate at your last picnic, or was it chipped beef? See the immense stock yards with their thousands of cattle, hogs and sheep, and think of the thousands of people that they feed. Cross the Missouri river and enter on the plains of the great and recently unknown west. Think of the pioneer who in 1849 traversed these once barren stretches of prairie, walking beside his slow-moving ox team, seeking the promised land, breaking a trail for the generations that were to come after him as you are coming now in a Pullman car . Think of the dangers that beset him on every hand, then wonder at the nerve he had, then again let your chest swell with pride that you are an American, sprung from the same stock that men were composed of in those days. Note the grandeur of the Rocky Mountains as they rise from the plains, their peaks snow-capped, glistening in clear blue sky, breathe the pure essence of life, drink of the crystal streams twinkling down their sides, then scorn the wine made by man. Listen to the salute of the bells and the whistles as the trains approach and pass that strange monument of nature's handiwork, the Mount of the Holy Cross.

Go to the Yellowstone National Park and revel in the wonders thereof, walk in the garden of the Gods and listen to the voice of the Giant Geyser as it sends forth its torrents of boiling water. Bathe in the life-giving springs and mud baths. Note the fantastic forms of the rocks and trees, carved by the hand of nature, then go to Colorado Springs and climb Pikes Peak and behold the world stretch out before you in valley, mountain and plain. Visit the mines of Leadville and Cripple Creek, the store houses of a part of the nation's wealth. Visit Denver and see the strides made in the improvement of the west in a short time. Board the Denver & Rio Grande train and note the magnificent scenery of mountain, canyons, gorges and the beautiful mountain lakes and streams, note the Grand Canyon of the Colorado, the royal gorge. Now note the great white expanse of the great Salt Lake, as it lies glistening in the rays of tile setting sun, and think of the stories you have heard of it until the conductor brings you back to earth with the cry of "Ogden."

Note this bustling railroad center in the heart of the Rocky mountains, and acknowledge our country's greatness. Visit Salt Lake City, the "City of Zion," the Canaan of the new world. See the beautiful city nestling within the protection of the Warsatch and Oquirrh range of mountains. Walk its wide tree-lined streets, visit the tabernacle and hear the sweet strains of the world's greatest organs. See the Mormon temple. Visit Saltair and sport in the waves of the briny sea. Board the San Pedro, Los Angeles and Salt Lake westbound train and cross the end of this same lake, one of nature's wonders.

Cross the desert of Nevada, which was only a short time ago a desert waste, on and on until you smell the orange blossoms of sunny California, and the train emerges from the mountains and brings into view the grand Pacific Ocean. See the big trees of California, the seals and the scenery of the Yosemite valley. Visit the orange groves and the vineyards, and partake of the orange and the grape. Visit Catalina Island in the Pacific Ocean, and try a couple of hours fishing in its waters. Then take the Southern Pacific and return to New York by way of Arizona, New Mexico, Texas, New Orleans, Florida and other southern states. Then again let your chest swell with pride that you are an American.

I think you will agree with me that this grand country of ours is the peer of any in the world, and that volumes cannot begin to tell of the wonders of it. Then after taking such a trip you will say with me, "See America." I have seen a large part of America, and am still seeing it, but the life of a hundred years would be all too short to see our country America, I love thee, Sweet land of Liberty, home of the brave and the free.

XXI

A Few of the Railroad Men Under Whom
I have Served. George M. Pullman.
The Town of Pullman, Ill. American Railroads
Lead the World. A Few Figures.

Among the large number of railroad men I have served under and
worked with during the fifteen years I have been on the road it
gives me pleasure to recall the names of a few with whom I was more
intimately acquainted and to whom I am indebted for many favors given
and courtesies extended, and the pleasant duty devolves on me to mention
the always courteous, obliging and most competent head of the Pullman
department in Denver, Mr. Runnells, and his assistant, Mr. Wright,
who sent me out on my first run in 1890. Next comes the well known
name of District Superintendent J. M. Smith, who one year later sent
me out on the run that marked the beginning of my Pullman service.
To Mr. Smith more than to any other railroad man I am indebted for
advice, counsel and countless favors shown me while I was in the service
in the department over which he presided so long. I always found him
courteous and obliging and never too busy to listen or to give a kind word
of advice or counsel to all who approached him on company business or
on the private affairs of the employees of the road. I had charge of a car
for several years in his territory and many a time I have had him for a
passenger and at such times he seemed more like an old friend than he
did like the superintendent of the Pullman service.

I next transferred to the Ogden division. Here I met and came
to know very well Superintendent Baker and his assistant, Johnnie
Searce, and to these two gentlemen I am also indebted for many favors
shown me, as they tried in every way possible to make my employment
pleasant and profitable while I was in their territory. I was sent out
on runs that covered the greater portions of the United States, and
while on some of my longer runs I often started from and returned
to stations in different districts under different superintendents, but
I always looked on Ogden as my home station and Superintendent
Baker as my chief until another superintendent was given charge of
the district and I transferred to Salt Lake and started to run on Senator
Clark's new road, the S. P., L. A. & S. L. road, between Salt Lake

and Los Angeles, under the superintendency of Mr. Twining and his assistant, Mr. Cotten, and these gentlemen also during the time I have been with them have shown me every favor and consideration, which goes far towards making my work a pleasure. In this connection also I mention the names of Jim Donohue, traveling engineer; W. H. Smith, trainmaster, and P. Randoff Morris and Jos. Jones, special agents, all jolly railroad men from A to Izard.

During my fifteen years' service I have met and served under many different superintendents and to mention the names of them all, would require a separate volume, but I will always hold them in kindly remembrance as they all have without exception been kindness itself to me.

Another old friend I have recently met on the steel road is William H. Blood, at present one of the popular conductors on the San Pedro, Los Angeles & Salt Lake Railroad. In the early seventies "Billy" was one of the best cowboys ranging over the western cattle country. He was with me on many of the old trails and in many a tight place, and like myself he always came out right side up with care and none the worse for wear.

E. W. Gillett, at present general passenger agent of the Salt Lake road, and one of the best known and most popular railroad men of the west, is another friend of the old days it is my pleasure to meet often now. I first met him under the following circumstances. I think it was in the year 1874 along in the fall, I had been up the trail with some cattle and was returning through Wyoming en route to Arizona. I had been riding hard all day and as it began to get dark I sighted a small station on the main line of the Union Pacific, and I concluded to give it a passing call out of curiosity. As I drew near I noticed several rough-looking customers hanging around in a suspicious manner, and I at once concluded that they were robbers there for the purpose of holding up the station. Events immediately following proved that I was right. They had not noticed me and they proceeded to hold up the agent in true western style, but that they had caught a tartar was evidenced by the rattle of the agent's artillery. Of course it was out of the question for me to miss such fun, so not waiting for an invitation I lost no time in getting my own forty-fives in active operation, and in less time than it takes to tell it what was left of those greasers were making tracks for the nearest state line, while a red-headed youngster with a smoking 45 in his fist was shaking hands with me and trying to say something about my saving his life. I took a shine to him at once on account of his pluck and our friendship thus begun has lasted through the years until now time and fate have thrown us both together on the same line of railroad.

The railroad men as a class are the most jovial set of men one could find in any profession, well educated, broad minded, and always considerate of others and at the same time they know their business thoroughly, as they have to serve many years as apprentices, so to speak, in railroading, before they are given places of trust and responsibility, and the man who has reached the position of president or general manager of a railroad system, has learned pretty much all there is to be learned about the iron horse and the steel road, and they use that knowledge in providing for the safety and comfort of the millions of lives that are annually intrusted to their keeping.

The general manager is responsible not only for the lives of the traveling public, but of the army or railroad employes under him and he is supposed to know everything, and must always be prepared to do the right thing in the right place at the right time, and as in many cases life and death depend on it, he must know how.

A college education does not make a railroad manager, although it may help to do so. He in a great measure gets his education in the school of experience, and in some cases it is a hard school, and the most exacting of all schools, but at the same time it is a school in which one can learn anything under the sun, and learn it well, and in these days of the twentieth century's activity and progress, it is the man who knows how to do things that makes the world move. And after boiling everything down there is left in the pot two undisputable facts. They are that the railroad men cause the world to move by knowing how to do things, the other is that the railroad men move the people who live in the world, thus they move things all around. And they are continually on the move themselves, which goes to prove that they are different from many other people inasmuch as they practice what they preach. And from these men of all classes from the president down I have received courtesies and the kindest of consideration, and these pleasant associations are pleasant memories to me and will always remain so.

It was my pleasure to meet and to chat with George M. Pullman, the father of the sleeping car, several times, and I found him to be a fine man, broad-minded in every sense of the word, always approachable and with always a kind word for every one of the large army of his employees that he met on his travels, and he always tried to meet them all. It was also my pleasure to meet his two boys who are veritable chips of the old block.

One of the legends connected with the western mining history is that early in the 60s George M. Pullman was a poor prospector and had secured a lease on a piece of mining ground in Colorado, and that he formed the idea of the sleeping car from the tiers of bunks in the miners' lodging house, "bunk houses" they are called. However that may be Mr. Pullman has been the recipient of many a blessing from the weary traveler, and the idea, whatever it was, that led him to invent the sleeping car that has proved such a comfort to the traveler of today, deserves to go down in history as the greatest idea that ever came from the place where ideas come from.

It has been my pleasure to visit all the large shops of the Pullman company, including the town of Pullman, Ill., which is a good-sized city, named after Mr. Pullman, and was owned by him principally, and the large number of men employed in his shops there. The town contains fine churches and public buildings, a splendid library and reading rooms and amusement halls. And while I was there I failed to see a single saloon. It seems such places are tabooed there. The shops are the finest in this country, containing all the modern machinery of the finest kind and the men employed there are all past masters of their trades. Here are built all the finest sleeping cars and many of the finest special cars and railway cars seen on the railroads of this country. In addition there is also a very large amount of repairing done. As soon as anything goes wrong with a Pullman car it is at once sent into the shops for repair, and soon comes out in apple pie order. You may see the Pullman cars all over this country where there is a steel road, and other countries have their eyes on the mof late, and in the near future it will be possible to sleep in a Pullman car whether you are traveling in England, France, Sweden or Cihna. They are a good thing and are sure to be pushed or rather pulled along.

In 1893 I went to Mr. Pullman and told him I was thinking of getting the porters of the Pullman Car Company to club together and contribute fifty cents per month apiece for the purpose of investing the proceeds in land, in view of eventually owning what we would call "The Porters' Home." Mr. Pullman told me he thought that a good idea, and said if we succeeded in buying one thousand acres of land, he would erect us a building on it, and signed a statement to that effect.

I then went to work and communicated with all the divisions of the Pullman Company, presenting this proposition to the porters of these different districts, but only succeeded in getting about twenty-five subscribers, the rest of them refusing to go into such a proposition, some of them saying all I wanted was to get the money and make away with it. Inasmuch as this amount was to be sent to the main Pullman office in Chicago and I was to be there each month to see this money deposited. Others refused to go into it upon the ground that they were liable to be discharged from the Pullman service at any time, and many other various excuses were offered. There were many of the Pullman conductors, however, who promised to contribute from one to five dollars toward this enterprise when we were ready to purchase the land.

My object was to have a Home and Hospital, with adjoining farming land, for the benefit of old and disabled porters who were not able to perform their duties as Pullman car porters. Had this been accomplished at that time, we would by now have had a large farm and a house and hospital connected therewith, and all the porters who are now unable to work would have had a good home and be cared for the rest of their lives. I hope to live long enough to yet see this plan become a reality.

At present the American railway leads the world. In no other country does the traveler find so much comfort, so many conveniences, so much pleasure, safety and speed as does the dweller in this robust young country belonging to our Uncle Samuel. At the present time there are in the United States upwards of two hundred and sixty thousand miles of railroad open and in operation, not to mention several thousand miles now building and projected. This immense mileage is divided between over one thousand different roads, while in 1851 there were only 149 different railroads with a total mileage of 9000 miles. The railroads today have a capital back of them amounting to over $14,000,000,000, and they pay their employees wages that foot up over $7,000,000 annually, while their earnings amount to the tidy sum of $2,500,000,000 in the same length of time. They carry somewhat more than 800,000,000 passengers every twelve months, and 2,200,000,000 tons of freight. These figures do not include the several million tons of trunks, sachels, grips, hat boxes and carpet bags that the average traveler considers it necessary to load him or herself down with on starting on a journey of any distance, and which comes in such large quantities sometimes as to make life a burden for us porters.

Read these figures again, dear reader, they are a conservative estimate of the business transacted by the railroads of this fair land of ours. You can count a million, can you count a billion? Immense, isn't it? It seems to show that the people of this country are great travelers, forever on the move, yet they tell us this is a country of homes and that the average American loves his home and home life above all things. These figures seem to show there are a few people who havn't any home or if they have they are looking for one they like better, which, like the will of the wisp, evades them always, but they continue to shift around, always hopeful, never satisfied, and they will continue to shift around until Gabriel blows on his little tin horn.

But this class of people make but a small percentage of the traveling public. Business in this latter day of strife and competition makes long journeys necessary, and as the business of the world grows apace and the countries of the earth crowd closer together in the struggle for the almighty dollar, there will be need of more railroads to make the globe smaller and to cut off the hours and minutes of precious time that means money to the man of today. And as a man makes and saves money so will he spend it for the pleasure of himself and family, and as he must travel to find pleasure there must be railroads to carry him, and hence these figures I write now will look insignificant beside the magnificent total that will be put before the reader of that day, because if they increase in the next century as they have in the past, walking will be out of fashion and every body will ride and I hope sleep in a Pullman sleeping car.

XXII

A Few Reminiscences of the Range. Some Men
I Have Met. Buffalo Bill. The James Brothers.
Yellowstone Kelley. The Murder of Buck Cannon by
Bill Woods. The Suicide of Jack Zimick.

It has now been many years since I quit the range, and as my mind wanders back over those years as it often does, memories both pleasant and sad pass in review and it is but fitting that I record a few of them as a final to the history of my life which has been so full of action, which is but natural as the men of those days were men of action. They had to be, and probably their actions were not all good, that I freely admit, but while that is so, it is equally so that their actions were not all bad, far from it. And in the history of the frontier there is recorded countless heroic deeds performed, deeds and actions that required an iron nerve, self denial in all that these words imply, the sacrificing of one life to save the life of a stranger or a friend. Deeds that stamped the men of the western plains as men worthy to be called men, and while not many of them would shine particularly in the polite society of today or among the 400 of Gotham, yet they did shine big and bright in the positions and at a time when men lived and died for a principle, and in the line of duty. A man who went to the far west or who claimed it as his home in the early days found there a life far different from that led by the dude of Fifth Avenue. There a man's work was to be done, and a man's life to be lived, and when death was to be met, he met it like a man. It was among such men and surroundings that I spent so many years of my life and there I met men some of whom are famous now, while others never lived long enough to reach the pinnacle of fame, but their memory is held no less sacred by the men who knew them well.

Some men I met in the cattle country are now known to the world as the baddest of bad men, yet I have seen these men perform deeds of valor, self sacrifice and kindness that would cause the deeds recorded as performed by gentlemen in "ye olden time when knighthood was in flower" to look insignificant in comparison, and yet these men lay no claim to the title of gentlemen. They were just plain men.

It was my pleasure to meet often during the early seventies the man who is now famous in the old world and the new world, Buffalo Bill (William F. Cody), cowboy, ranger, hunter, scout and showman, a man who carried his life in his hands day and night in the wild country where duty called, and has often bluffed the grim reaper Death to a standstill, and is living now, hale, hearty and famous.

Others who are equally famous but in another way are the James brothers, Jesse and Frank. I met them often in the old days on the range, and became very well acquainted with them and many others of their band. Their names are recorded in history as the most famous robbers of the new world, but to us cowboys of the cattle country who knew them well, they were true men, brave, kind, generous and considerate, and while they were robbers and bandits, yet what they took from the rich they gave to the poor. The James brothers band stole thousands of dollars; yet Jesse was a poor man when he fell a victim to the bullet of a cowardly, traitorous assassin, and Frank James is a poor man today. What then did they do with the thousands they stole? The answer is simple, they gave it away to those who were in need. That is why they had so many friends and the officers of the law found it so hard to capture them.

And if they were robbers, by what name are we to call of the great trusts, corporations and brokers, who have for years been robbing the people of this country, some of them, I am glad to say, are now behind prison bars, still others are even now piling up the dollars that they have been and are still stealing from the American people, and who on account of these same dollars are looked up to, respected and are honored members of society, and the only difference between them and the James brothers is that the James brothers stole from the rich and gave to the poor, while these respected members of society steal from the poor to make the rich richer, and which of them think you reader, will get the benefit of the judgment when the final day arrives and all men appear before the great white throne in final judgment?

Jessie James was a true man, a loving son and husband, true to his word, true to his principles and true to his comrads and his friends. I had the pleasure of meeting Frank James quite recently on the road while he was en route to the coast with his theatrical company and enjoyed a pleasant chat with him. He knew me and recalled many incidents of the old days and happenings in "no man's land."

Quite a different sort of man was Yellowstone Kelley, government scout, hunter and trapper. He was one of the men who helped to make frontier history and open up the pathless wilds to the march of civilization. He was in the employ of the government as a scout and guide when I first met him, and thereafter during our many wanderings over the country, I with my cattle, he with Uncle Sam's soldiers or on a lone scout, we often bumped up against each other, and these meetings are among my treasured memories. He was a man who knew the country better than he knew his own mother, absolutely fearless, kind and generous to a fault. He was the sort of a man that once you meet him you could never forget him, and us boys who knew him well considered him the chief of all the government scouts of that day. I also had the pleasure of meeting Kit Carson in Arizona and nearly all the government scouts, hunters and trappers of the western country, and they can all be described in one sentence, they were men whom it was a pleasure and an honor to know.

"Billie the Kid" was another sort of a man and there has never been another man like him and I don't think there ever will be again. Writers claim that he was a man all bad. This I doubt as I knew him well and I have known him to do deeds of kindness. He had many traits that go to make a good man, but fate and circumstances were against the kid, yet I know he always remembered a kindness done him and he never forgave an enemy. I have rode by his side many a long mile, and it is hard to believe he was as bad as he is pictured to be, but the facts are against him, and when his career was ended by the bullet from Sheriff Garrett's colt, the world was better off, likewise were some men who stood in mortal fear of the kid, and I suppose they had good reason to be afraid as the kid always kept his word.

During my employment with the Duval outfit and Pete Gallingan I often made trips on the trail with herds of cattle and horses belonging to other ranch owners, and on these trips many incidents occurred, amusing and sad. The following incident happened in the fall of 1878, when I went up the trail with the half circle box brand outfit, belonging to Arthur Gorman and company.

We had a small herd of horses to take to Dodge City, where we arrived after an uneventful trip, and after disposing of the horses we started but to do the town as usual. But in this we met an unexpected snag. Our bookkeeper, Jack Zimick, got into a poker game and lost all the money he had to pay the cowboys off with, which amounted to about two thousand dollars, and also about the same amount of the boss' money. The boys had about one and a half years' wages coming to them, and consequently they were in a rather bad humor when they heard this bit of news. They at once got after Zimick so hard that he took me and went to Kinsely, Kas., where Mr. Gorman was. Arriving there he went to the Smith saloon to get a room, as Smith ran a rooming house over his saloon, and it was the custom for all the cattle men to make it their headquarters when in the city. Here he met Mr. Gorman, and we were sitting around the room and Zimick had only told Mr. Gorman a few things, when all of a sudden Zimick drew his 45 colt revolver remarking as he did so, "Here is the last of Jack Zimick." He placed the gun to his head and before we could reach him he pulled the trigger, and his brains were scattered all over the room.

They arrested Mr. Gorman and myself and held up for a short time until things could be explained. Mr. Gorman was very much overcome by the act, as Jack was one of his best men, and had been with him a long time. Mr. Gorman had the body sent to Zimick's friends in Boston, and he personally paid off all the boys, taking the money out of his own pocket to do so, but when the boys heard of Jack's rash deed they said they would rather have lost every dollar they had, rather than have had Jack kill himself, as he was a favorite among all the cowboys, especially so among those in Mr. Gorman's employ. Zimick had been in the employ of Gorman and company for over ten years and he was Mr. Gorman's right hand man, and this was the first time he ever went wrong. Jack did not have the nerve to face his comrades again, and so I suppose he concluded that his colt 45 was the only friend he had to help him out of it.

In May 1882, I was in Durango, Colorado, and chanced to be in a saloon on Main street where a lot of us boys were together, among them being Buck Cannon and Bill Woods. The drinks had been circulating around pretty freely when Cannon and Woods got into a dispute over Cannon's niece, to whom Woods had been paying attention, much against that young lady's wish. After some hot words between the men, Woods drew his 45 colt revolver, remarking as he did so, "I will kill you," and in raising it his finger must have slipped, as his gun went off and the bullet hit a glass of beer in the hand of a man who was in the act of raising it to his lips, scattering the broken glass all over the room, then passing through the ceiling of the saloon. In an instant Woods threw three bullets into Cannon, remarking as he did so, "I will kill you, for your niece is my heart's delight and I will die for here." Buck Cannon's dying words were, "Boys, don't let a good man die with his boots on."

Along in the spring of 1879 we sent to Dodge City, Kansas, with a herd of cattle for the market and after they were disposed of, we boys turned our attention to the search of amusement. Some of the boys made for the nearest saloon and card table, but I heard there was to be a dance at Bill Smith's dance hall and in company with some of the other boys decided to attend. There was always quite a large number of cowboys in Dodge City at this time of the year, so we were not surprised to find the dance hall crowded on our arrival there. Smith's place occupied a large, low frame building down by the railroad tracks on the south. We found many old acquaintances there, among them being Kiowa Bill, a colored cattle man and ranch owner of Kansas, whose ranch was on Kiowa creek. I had met him several times but this was the first time I had seen him in a couple of years, but as he was dancing with a young lady I could not get to speak with him at once. So I looked up a wall flower and proceeded to enjoy myself. We had not been dancing long when I became aware of a commotion over near the bar, and all eyes were turned in that direction. I soon ascertained the cause of the commotion to be a dispute between Kiowa Bill and Bill Smith, the proprietor of the place, who was behind the bar. Kiowa Bill, after finishing the dance with his fair partner, took her to the bar to treat her. Smith, who was tending bar refused to serve her saying she had enough already. Kiowa Bill told Smith he (Kiowa Bill) was paying for what she wanted to drink and that he wanted her to get what she wanted. Smith said no, she could not have anything more to drink as she had too much already. At this Kiowa Bill reached over the bar and struck Smith over the head with a whiskey bottle, partly stunning him, but he recovered in an instant and grabbed his 45 Colt, Kiowa Bill doing the same and both guns spoke as one. Smith fell dead behind the bar with a bullet through his heart. Kiowa Bill rolled against the bar and slowly sank to the floor and was dead when we reached him.

The next day they were hauled to the cemetery, laying side by side in the same wagon, and were buried side by side in the same grave. Kiowa Bill had made his will a short time before and it was found on his body when he was killed.

I had known Kiowa Bill for several years and was present at a shooting scrape he had two years before, down in Texas, near the Arizona line. At one of the big round ups there, in 1877, myself and quite a crowd of the other boys were in camp eating our dinner when Kiowa Bill rode up. He had been looking after his own cattle as he owned over two thousand head himself. One of the boys in our party who did not like Bill, there being a feud between them for sometime, on noticing Bill approaching, remarked, "If that fellow comes here I will rope him." True to his work as Bill rode up, the cowboy threw his lariat. Kiowa Bill, seeing the movement, threw the rope off at the same time springing down on the opposite side of his horse.

The cowboy, enraged at his failure to rope Bill, shouted, "I will fight you from the point of a jack knife, to the point of a 45," at the same time reaching for his 45 which was in the holster on his saddle, which was lying on the ground a short distance away. At that Kiowa Bill fired, striking the cowboy in the neck, breaking it. Bill then sprang in the saddle and put spurs to his horse in an effort to get away.

Several of the cowboys commenced shooting after Bill who returned the fire. One of the cowboys, squatting down and holding his 45 with both hands, in an effort to get a better aim on Bill, received a bullet in the leg from Bill's revolver that knocked him over backwards, and caused him to turn a couple of somersaults. Bill got away and went to New York. He was later arrested in St. Louis and brought back. At his trial he went free as it was shown that be killed the cowboy in self-defense. And his appearance at the dance was the first time I had seen him since the scrape in Texas.

Kiowa Bill was of a peaceful disposition and always refrained from bothering with others, but if others bothered with him they were liable to get killed as Kiowa Bill allowed no one to monkey with him. Such was life on the western ranges when I rode them, and such were my comrades and surroundings; humor and tragedy. In the midst of life we were in death, but above all shown the universal manhood. The wild and free life. The boundless plains. The countless thousands of long horn steers, the wild fleet footed mustangs. The buffalo and other game, the Indians, the delight of living, and the fights against death than caused every nerve to tingle, and the every day communion with men, whose minds were as broad as the plains they roamed, and whose creed was every man for himself and every friend for each other, and with each other till the end.

Another friend of the old times is Chas. R. Campbell, superintendent of the Kelso mines. Chats with these good whole-souled people of the cattle range bring back reminiscences of the past that would fill volumes but space and time in these days of hustle and bustle are but dreams and the world is full of them now.

I am at the present time connected with the General Securities Company in Los Angeles. Mr. A. A. C. Ames is president; Mr. James O. Butler, vice-president; Mr. Jacob E. Meyer, secretary, and Mr. Geo. W. Bishop, treasurer. These gentlemen are always extremely kind to me and the appreciation I feel for the kindnesses shown me will be fully rewarded.

As I stop to ponder over the days of old so full of adventure and excitement, health and happiness, love and sorrow, isn't it a wonder that some of us are alive to tell the tale. One moment we are rejoicing that we are alive; the next we are so near the jaws of death that it seems it would be almost a miracle that our lives be saved.

Life today on the cattle range is almost another epoch. Laws have been enacted in New Mexico and Arizona which forbid all the old-time sports and the cowboy is almost a being of the past. But, I, Nat Love, now in my 54th year, hale hearty and happy, will ever cherish a fond and loving feeling for the old days on the range, its exciting adventures, good horses, good and bad men, long venturesome rides, Indian fights and last but foremost the friends I have made and friends I have gained.

FINIS

A Note About the Author

Nat Love (1854–1921) was an African American cowboy. Born into slavery on the plantation of Robert Love in Tennessee, Love learned to read and write at a young age despite the criminalization of black literacy throughout the South. Following emancipation, his parents remained on the plantation as sharecroppers until Sampson, his father, died unexpectedly. Forced to grow up fast, Love worked as a breaker of horses on a local farm and managed to earn enough to leave town by the age of 16. He headed West via Kansas, working as a cowboy along the way. Love excelled as a cattle driver, fighting off rustlers and learning how to shoot and survive in the harsh American wilderness. Throughout his travels, he met Pat Garrett and Billy the Kid, became a prizewinning rodeo star, and was captured by a group of Pima Indians. He eventually settled in California, where he published his autobiography *The Life and Adventures of Nat Love* (1907) and worked as a courier and guard for a Los Angeles firm.

A Note from the Publisher

Spanning many genres, from non-fiction essays to literature classics to children's books and lyric poetry, Mint Edition books showcase the master works of our time in a modern new package. The text is freshly typeset, is clean and easy to read, and features a new note about the author in each volume. Many books also include exclusive new introductory material. Every book boasts a striking new cover, which makes it as appropriate for collecting as it is for gift giving. Mint Edition books are only printed when a reader orders them, so natural resources are not wasted. We're proud that our books are never manufactured in excess and exist only in the exact quantity they need to be read and enjoyed. To learn more and view our library, go to minteditionbooks.com

bookfinity & ![MINT EDITIONS] MINT EDITIONS

Enjoy more of your favorite classics with Bookfinity,
a new search and discovery experience for readers.
With Bookfinity, you can discover more vintage
literature for your collection, find your Reader Type,
track books you've read or want to read,
and add reviews to your favorite books.
Visit www.bookfinity.com, and click on
Take the Quiz to get started.

Don't forget to follow us
@bookfinityofficial and @mint_editions

CPSIA information can be obtained
at www.ICGtesting.com
Printed in the USA
LVHW081418261121
704536LV00002B/311